The Organizational Sweet Spot

Charles Ehin
Westminster College
Salt Lake City, UT
USA

ISBN 978-0-387-98193-2   e-ISBN 978-0-387-98194-9
DOI 10.1007/978-0-387-98194-9
Springer Dordrecht Heidelberg London New York

Library of Congress Control Number: 2009927721

Printed on acid-free paper

Springer is part of Springer Science+Business Media (www.springer.com)

To Franz Böge and Hank Rumana,
the mentors I will never forget!

Acknowledgments

When sitting down to write a paper or a book, I invariably ask myself, "Why do you want to take the time and effort to put this piece together?" It's not only the time and effort that must be devoted to such a task, but it's also the mental and physical agony that one must endure sitting for hours at a time with a laptop, not just writing but debating with yourself, wanting to make sure that you are heading down the right path. Of course, that debate seldom ends with a firm affirmation of the questions posed.

There is usually, however, something internal that compels me to press on. I also keep going because of the encouragements I receive from my extended family, friends, and colleagues. Some of these people are part of memories of relationships long past, including acquaintances no longer among the living. The bottom line is that no matter who you are and what you do, life is founded on relationships past, present, and those still beyond the horizon.

This book is based on a compilation of ideas and mental models whose bits and pieces have whirled around in my mind for decades, going back to the days immediately after the end of World War II when I was completing my elementary school education in Hamburg-Bergedorf, Germany. That is why this work, as well as the others I have written, is not purely about management or business. It is more about life itself.

As a result, I begin my acknowledgements with several names from the past. Franz Böge and Hank Rumana immediately come to mind first. Herr Böge was my most memorable elementary school teacher in Hamburg-Bergedorf, although I had begun my primary education in my native country, Estonia, several years before. Somehow he had managed to survive the misery and hunger of Russian gulags as a prisoner of war. He walked with a slight limp caused by wounds he had suffered in combat. Already a school teacher before the war, he was elated to be back in the classroom.

Herr Böge was a teacher's teacher. He was a strict disciplinarian, but he loved his students and did everything possible to make learning meaningful and inspiring. History, for example, was taught as much outside of the classroom as inside. We visited museums and ancient historic sites all around Hamburg. But that was only part of a lesson. As homework we then had to draw pictures and write short papers about what we had discovered and learned. Of course, those homework assignments were also freely shared in class. The curiosity about the world around me that this man helped to unleash within me has not subsided to this day.

Hank Rumana was my high school football coach and much more than just a great mentor. He essentially became my second father. He helped me to believe in myself and realize my potential, not only as an athlete but also as a scholar. He also aided me in honing my initial relationship skills as I worked as a head counselor in his boy's summer camp. Likewise, he encouraged me to attend either Colgate or Princeton rather than accept scholarship offers from numerous other larger nationally recognized institutions. I chose Colgate University.

This book is dedicated to Franz Böge and Hank Rumana. My close relationships with these two compassionate and farsighted individuals gave me a solid personal foundation that has lasted to this day. There is no question that without their fatherly care my life would have taken a much different and less fulfilling track.

I have had, of course, many other important relationships that have impacted my life extensively. At Colgate my philosophy professor, Dr. R.V. Smith, taught me to always keep a keen eye between assumptions and facts. Later working with Frederick Herzberg, the noted academician and motivation theory guru, I began to comprehend that motivation, like relationships, was an emergent personal dynamic quite separate from supervision or organizational contexts.

In the past 3 years a number of individuals, primarily those who are frequent participants on the Google Value-Networks, have also added considerably to my thinking and helped to clarify certain ill-defined points of contention. They include Verna Allee, John Maloney, Dave Snowden, Jay Deragon, and many others too numerous to name. All these folks are "pushing the envelope" in the area of emergence and complex evolving systems where the topic of relationships also belongs.

Three people deserve special credit for making this work possible. I owe a great deal of gratitude to Nicholas (Nick) Philipson, the Senior Editor of Business and Economics at Springer. Nick and I established a solid relationship several years ago when I was looking for a home for *Hidden Assets*, my second management book. At the time he was working for another publisher. So, I was pleasantly surprised when Nick responded to my query at Springer about this manuscript. To say the least, he is one of the most engaging and pleasant people to work with. He is always ready to help, but at the same time is very frank about the quality of one's research and writing. His guidance has been extremely helpful in bringing this work to fruition.

Another is Lynn Allen, a longtime friend who volunteered to edit the book. She was absolutely magnificent in making suggestions about how to make the manuscript more readable. She also posed questions that led to the expansion of several portions of the text to clarify certain important concepts and models.

Last but foremost, I am enormously indebted to the love of my life, my wife Betty, for her moral support in moments when it seemed senseless to me to continue writing and when emotions seemed to have gotten the better of me. She has always been the "cool head" in our partnership, keeping a lid on this old Estonian. Our wondrous relationship has prospered for more than a half a century.

Contents

Chapter 1
Introduction: Closing the Engagement Gap

A pervasive and costly condition is smothering almost one fifth of the US workforce.

This condition affects about 24.7 million US workers. It causes lethargy, apathy, negativity, and occasional disruptions in appetite and sleeping patterns. Another common symptom is the inability to concentrate on routine tasks that naturally results in reduced productivity.

To make matters worse, this affliction costs the US economy anywhere from $292 billion to $355 billion annually.

Corporate managers and budget officers are understandably concerned, but they are seemingly unable to do anything to change or reduced this condition's effects on their workplaces or their corporations' bottom lines. In fact, many of them are not only unaware of how to fix it, but they are also unwilling to do what's necessary to turn it around.

Science fiction? No. It's real.

Epidemic? Maybe.

Pervasive and costly? Yes, absolutely. But what is this workplace condition and why haven't we heard about it? If it were a disease, it would be declared a national emergency and a massive effort initiated to contain the epidemic. The entire world would pay attention.

The condition? *Active employee disengagement.*

The actively disengaged are people who are physically at their place of work, yet mentally are miles away, immersed in any activity that is more meaningful and satisfying to them than their jobs. They are very likely those who search personal interests on the Internet or talk at length in nonwork related phone conversations. They're happy to do anything that has nothing to do with their jobs or the business at hand.

Fortunately, this is not a physical disease. Unfortunately, it continues to sap our workforce and rob our economy.

In January 2008, a national Gallup Q12 Employee Engagement Survey found that about 24.7 million workers in the US workforce are almost completely disconnected from their jobs. That's 19% – almost one in five of American workers – who don't care, don't like, and probably skimp on their jobs. Is there any wonder the cost is so high?

C. Ehin, *The Organizational Sweet Spot: Engaging the Innovative Dynamics of Your Social Networks*,
DOI 10.1007/978-0-387-98194-9_1, © Springer Science+Business Media, LLC 2009

Disengagement is not isolated to the USA. In Germany, various surveys found that between 79 and 90% of employees don't think their day-to-day work has any impact on their future salary or career opportunities. They too are disengaged.

Let's explore the numbers to get a feel for the financial impact disengagement has on organizations. Dividing the $355 billion lost by the total of the US workforce of about 130 million people averages out to *$2,730 lost per worker each year.* Not just disengaged workers, but all workers. Adding in the cost of "partially" disengaged employees to the equation drives the cost even higher.

No matter how you look at this situation, it's adding considerable nonproductive expense to every enterprise nationwide.

Can you imagine how much could be saved by just spending $500 per worker per year to minimize the disengagement problem? Not only would people become more productive at what they are doing, but they would also add considerably more to the overall innovative capacity of an organization.

Two questions arise from this scenario. The first is "Why are so many workers actively disengaged from their jobs?" It's tempting to look for answers in such disheartening issues such as the decreasing relative wages of the middle-class workers, promises of bonuses that go unpaid, and employee surveys that produce either no results or hostile work environments.

All these issues certainly have an impact and many organizations try to fix disengagement by tweaking processes and systems. Computer networking, motivational training, right-sizing, and internal reorganization are among the many methods used to address the problems. Managers keep trying one new process or technology after another in the search for the Holy Grail of Management or the "perfect organization."

But these quests are more often exercises in futility addressing the symptoms of the problem and not the cause; they will not succeed. They will inevitably show their imperfections, leading to wave after wave of new programs and system interventions. As each wave crashes on the "beaches of organizations" with little improvement, managers are left with a second nagging question: "If our system still doesn't function well after numerous adjustments and our employees show little or no engagement, then how does any work get done at all?"

The source of the problem is too deep-seated to be solved by merely tweaking a system. Employee disengagement appears to happen because most people in leadership positions are out of touch with human nature, especially regarding work relationships. For the most part, the relationships formed between employees are discounted as not valuable or necessary, or even worse, they are discouraged. It never occurs to management that a large part of the solution is allowing human nature to play out organically in the work place, especially our intrinsic need to form useful work relationships.

First, let's briefly examine the nature of underlying systems most closely.

Doc Searls (2007, December 26, Weblog), the Senior Editor of the *Linux Journal,* briefly describes the fundamental problem and dynamics of the predicament as an imbalance in three aspects of organizational functions he terms "markets": transaction, conversation, and relationship.

> Think of markets as three overlapping circles: Transaction, Conversation and Relationship. Our financial system is Transaction run amok. Metastasized. Optimized at all costs. Impoverished in the Conversation department, and dismissive of Relationship entirely. We've been systematically eliminating Relationship for decades, excluding, devaluing and controlling human interaction wherever possible, to maximize efficiency and mechanization.

Searls asserts here that we ignore the most fundamental of human engagement dynamics, particularly relationships, and their interdependence in many of our organizations primarily in favor of transactions and curtailed conversations.

Managers are particularly clueless when it comes to the importance of close personal relationships in the innovation process or virtuous cycles. Research shows that this innate human predisposition to connect takes precedence over any organizational goals and profit motives advocated by business leaders.

Yet most administrators seem to disregard people's relentless instinctive drive to find and keep their personal and group identities in favor of "growing the business" or increasing the bottom line. Many managers still seem to doubt that "soft" human dynamics as relationships can have significant value and impact, especially on business functions.

The cost for that oversight is enormous both financially and in terms of worker despair. We are completely discarding the emotions and innovative ideas of almost 25 million people. What an unimaginable waste of human potential.

The importance of reversing these losses is compelling. Developing organizational contexts that close, or at least narrow, the social engagement gap are obviously a major factor in reengaging our workforce.

Placing greater emphasis on enhancing relationships that evolve within our organizations will be a big step in the right direction. If we can improve the nature of relationship at work, then most people will be more inclined to want to improve their organization's productivity and competitive advantage. Coevolving relationships are not only extremely important to every employee, but also they have a significant impact on organizational success and profitability.

But how should this be understood and accomplished within our organizations? How do we begin to tackle this huge worker disengagement gap?

The Grand Myth

Let's set the stage by first identifying the greatest management myth ever conceived and perpetuated on humans. It's an age-old myth originating about 10,000 BC, evidenced by the administrative and military structures of large societies that evolved after the advent of the agricultural revolution. The myth gained peak support millennia later during the Industrial Revolution of the 1800s and still is high on the "things to do" list of many executives and management consultants.

Ironically, there is no anthropological evidence that our kind used such constructs for roughly 200,000 years prior to the beginning of the agricultural revolution. But just for comparison, let's look at a simplified model:

Fig. 1.1 Organizational relationship myth

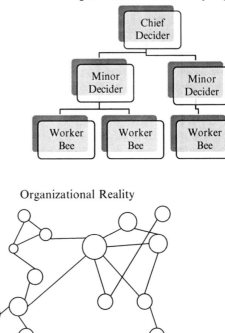

Organizational Relationship Myth

Organizational Reality

Fig. 1.2 Organizational reality

The Grand Organizational Myth as depicted by Fig. 1.1 is based on the notion that human social systems get things done through linear, mechanical, top-down structures. The fact that an organizational chart is almost always included in new hire packets is testament to the ubiquity of the Myth.

Most organizations still rigidly adhere to the time-honored assumptions that it's possible to (1) manage and predict the outcomes of social systems, and (2) develop optimal organizational frameworks. Both are unfortunate delusions.

Fortunately, experience and research is slowly beginning to chip away at the facade and openly reveal what most sage individuals have known for ages: social systems really don't work that way.

Social systems are organic, not mechanistic. They are composed of vibrant, constantly evolving, self-regulating networks. They don't look or perform like "machines." In fact, social systems *work in spite of and around* mechanical structures, whether those structures are devised by heads of prison administrators or managers set on running very "strictly disciplined" organizations. Figure 1.2 is a more realistic portrayal of how work gets done in most organizations.

Feel familiar? It should.

The next obvious question is, "Why don't groups conform to formal structures, directives, or policies precisely as planned?"

The simple answer is that it's physiologically and psychologically impossible for any person or group to respond to external demands (such as a directive or a certain work context) exactly as intended.

Why? Because of all the billions of people that have lived or now live on this planet, no two people have ever been genetically or experientially identical. Even identical twins are not 100% the same. Therefore, no individual or group can look at a directive (or anything else) and see it exactly as another individual or group sees it.

In addition, people innately hook up with individuals and social networks that they believe have the same general goals and interests. These emergent support groups also have their own interpretations of what is pertinent and how various processes should be handled.

That's why no matter how determined some administrators are to manage or control people and no matter what sorts of ingenious organizational frameworks they use to manage them, in reality it's an impossible task. These systems can't and don't allow for the vital and variable component of relationship.

The bottom line is that organizational parameters can be adjusted or managed, but the precise behavioral outcomes of the people within those structures, can't be.

Each chapter that follows will progressively build upon this reality to arrive at a new way of thinking and implementing management. Rather than learning how to control the structure, we will explore how to create an environment where these vital, nuanced, and somewhat chaotic relationships can flourish for the benefit of not only the individuals involved, but also the organization as a whole.

Scope

This book explores meaningful answers to the two fundamental questions asked earlier: "Why are so many workers in the United States actively disengaged from their jobs?" and "If our system still doesn't function well after numerous adjustments, and our employees show little or no engagement, then how does any work get done at all?"

The answers will not be another idyllic management theory. Instead we'll explore the principles of complex adaptive systems, or self-organization, and the latest research findings from social neuroscience and social network analysis. For this reason, the focus of this work is primarily on *emergent social systems.* Essentially these are social entities that form, function, and thrive without supervision. It's all about the power of social engagement and self-organization instead of continuous attempts to control people.

My research and experience suggests that relationships are the very life blood of successful social entities and the cycles of innovation within them. Relationships are also fundamental as we develop and maintain our individual and group identities. To access this powerful resource, we need to reach beyond transactions and conversations within and beyond our organizations. After all, we are dealing with the talents and skills of human beings who are intrinsically self-sustaining creatures that didn't evolve to be "managed" by others.

The most unique aspect explained in this work is a clear demonstration of the specific differences between the formal and informal social systems that are part of every business venture. In fact, I do something that has yet to be suggested by any other source. I pinpoint the "sweet spot" or what I have labeled the "shared-access domain" where the formal and the informal elements of an organization overlap.

It is here where individuals from both sides voluntarily form new (emergent) groups to solve problems. The sweet spot is precisely where most of the productive work in a business takes place. It is this domain with its uncontrollable dynamics that needs our utmost attention if we are to unleash the innovative ideas of the people within our organized endeavors.

Thus, allowing the shared-access domain to expand by NOT managing it, leads directly to positive relationships and increased innovation. We will explore in nonprescriptive terms how best to zero in on this organizational sweet spot.

My approach is nonprescriptive because each social entity is composed of different people and held together by dissimilar dynamics/chemistry even if they are producing identical products or services. That's why no one can precisely stipulate how a group should carry out its functions other than the members of the group itself. This fact will become clearer in the chapters that follow.

You may also notice the lack of existing organizational examples, or benchmarks, in this book. The rationale for that is quite simple: the focus of this work is primarily on "emergent" social systems rather than already existing ones. We are striving for a complete, more engaged, and forward looking style of unmanagement. Looking backward will not be useful.

Benchmarks provide good history lessons. But since history almost never repeats itself, trying to exactly copy a benchmark won't get you very far. What worked for a friend or competitor is unique to their organization and most likely won't fit others. Besides, emergent systems arise naturally out of their own environment. The most meaningful payoffs are usually found in exceptions and differences, but not in imitations.

Enterprises are composed of people who are impulsive about goals, feelings, and actions at least as often as they are rational. Toss into the mix a constantly changing environment and it doesn't take a genius to see that organizational predictability just isn't in the cards. Anything describing a "predictable" organization is pure fiction. They simply don't exist. Something within and without will always be changing.

To survive amid such chaos, a viable organization will need to greet each day with fresh vigor instead of standard routines. Also, each member of an enterprise will need to be prepared to evaluate the risks of alternative futures in the pursuit of current goals and objective. Further, as Verna Allee (2003, p. 242) aptly suggests, "…for maximum benefits all the participants need to understand how the whole system is working, so they can fully participate, gain the greatest value, yet help maintain integrity of the whole."

Agenda

We'll first examine three key social engagement elements mentioned earlier: transactions, conversations, and relationships. I've developed 21 models to help illustrate how they all work.

Then, we'll look at the four most central factors critical for the development of positive, constructive relationships — self-organization, tacit knowledge, social capital, and human nature. We'll see how the interplay between all these components impact innovation at the individual, dyad (two people), and group levels.

We'll conclude with recommendations for using several descriptive (experience-based) rather than prescriptive (rule-based or absolute) general principles for developing flexible organizational environments where social engagement and innovation are not only possible, but also probable. In other words, we'll look at the basic ingredients for forging organizations that encourage and maximize talents, ideas, and innovation through relationships – organizations that engage rather than disengage their employees.

In Chap. 2, we'll investigate the four key dynamic elements or mainstays of human interactions: transactions, conversation, relationships, and individual and group identities. You'll be introduced to the concept of the organizational "sweet spot" or "shared-access domain" located between the formal and informal sides of the organization as an overlapping merge point.

The focus in Chap. 3 is on a fundamental social process and three key relationship factors. Here we'll look at the deep-seated process of self-organization that governs the activities of all living entities. The three relationship factors discussed are evolved human predispositions, tacit knowledge, and social capital.

Chapter 4 covers the virtuous cycle dynamics that lead to expanded innovation capacities at both the individual and organizational levels. Also explored are two divergent organizational contexts and their attributes associated with relationship and identity development.

The focal point in Chap. 5 is on "catalytic" leadership akin to value-added knowledge facilitation rather than the currently in-vogue hierarchical models. We'll also briefly review some of the past and current leadership theories and their attributes.

The spotlight in Chap. 6 is on the development and maintenance of flexible and supportive social network ecosystems. We'll also examine the interrelationships and dynamics of key organizational success factors.

In the Epilogue, we'll reexamine the innovative power of social engagement and why we need to focus on its key element of relationships as the vital component in closing the engagement gap in the US workforce and revitalizing our commercial arena.

References

Allee, V. (2003) *The Future of Knowledge*. Boston: Butterworth-Heinemann.
Ehin, C. (2000) *Unleashing Intellectual Capital*. Boston: Butterworth-Heinemann.
Searls, D. (2007) *Weblog*, December 26.

Chapter 2
Mainstays of Social Engagements

Let's take a closer look at Searls' interdependent market features: transactions, conversations, and relationships. These market features are the mainstays of social engagement and are present in individual and group identity dynamics. Figure 2.1 depicts the interdependence of the three factors.

This model can also be a tool for observing social engagement at any level. It's appropriate for not only the interactions of two individuals, but also working teams, entire organizations, and extended worldwide networks. You can even apply this model to how individual identities develop and are maintained.

Searls' conceptual framework is an ingenious means for assessing the extent of engagement in any collaborative effort. Throughout the book the focus will be on the relationship aspect of the model, the most ignored market or engagement component in nearly all management systems.

Transactions are exchanges of tangible or intangible items between two or more parties. They can include monetary attributes such as stocks, tangibles such as machinery, intangibles such as patents, or all the three factors.

The point to remember is that no matter what a transaction includes, it's always explicit whether there's a signed agreement or not. The process is easily traced because an event or several events must take place before a transaction is completed.

The same is true for *conversations*. At least two people, by whatever means, have to exchange ideas or stories for a conversation to take place. Transactions and conversations are both *explicit*, even under highly informal circumstances. In other words, they are specific, definable, and fully developed. They also have an explicit value whether economic, intellectual, emotional, or spiritual.

Not so with *relationship*. Because relationships are based on spontaneity and intimacy, two commodities that cannot be traced, relationships are *implicit*. Unlike transactions and conversations, they are not solid or definable. By their very nature, they exist because of unexpressed agreement or affinity which is difficult, if not impossible, to define. This implicit nature is a major difference between relationship and the other two features.

Relationships also can have intrinsic value in the same ways as transactions and conversations. However, since relationships are implicit, the values derived from them develop over time and are not necessarily the initial foundations for the associations.

C. Ehin, *The Organizational Sweet Spot: Engaging the Innovative Dynamics of Your Social Networks*,
DOI 10.1007/978-0-387-98194-9_2, © Springer Science+Business Media, LLC 2009

Fig. 2.1 Social engagement dynamics

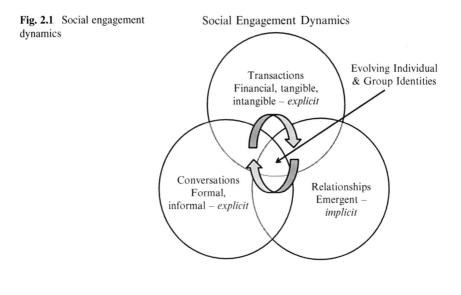

Social Engagement Dynamics

Relationships and individual identities are constantly evolving for better or for worse, depending on the biophysical and social contexts. It's an unplanned, self-organizing process between two or more parties where the outcomes are unpredictable. Given their implicit, unpredictable nature, relationships can be influenced but not controlled by third parties or varying *environmental contexts.*

The key point to remember is that because relationships and identities arise naturally, they are *emergent*. Since organizations are generally populated by at least two or more individuals, relationships will arise with all their delightful volatility and variations, no matter what type of organization you consider. Relationships are the informal social fabric of every organization and network whether we are dealing with a neighborhood book club, the office grapevine, or the United Nations.

Circular Causality

Since individuals are rarely truly isolated, it is useful to look at an explanation of circular causality. In this model, you can come to see the importance of relationships on an individual's as well as a group's development.

In the old linear model, person A does something to person B who then causes something else to happen to person C – all in a straight, predictable fashion. This busy manager's dream team is illustrated in Fig. 2.2.

When it comes to people and relationships, however, this tidy arrangement rarely happens. In reality, the linear model of cause and effect is not particularly useful when it comes to people.

Individuals are seldom in total isolation. It makes sense that to observe or understand someone, you must also look at the interrelationships within their social world.

Fig. 2.2 Cause and effect relationships

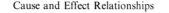

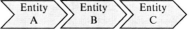

What you find is that rather than being linear and static, cause and effect in relationships is circular and changes constantly as relationships change and reorganize of their own accord.

The concept of circular causality, or self-organization, is much more accurate when it comes to analyzing relationships (see Fig. 3.1).

In this case, when person A affects person B in some fashion, B is also a cause, and can turn around and affect or change the behavior in person A, and so on. The more persons A and B interact, the more opportunity they have to affect or change each other. They naturally evolve as a result of the interactions they have with each other. Add persons C and D, and the opportunities for mutually influencing and changing each other increase even more.

We instinctively know that a person or group has an intrinsic, naturally evolving ability to modify itself as situations shift or the group's membership changes. The dynamics of relationships are founded on circular causality or self-organization, which we'll discuss more fully Chap 3.

Individual Identities

The first logical step in exploring the nature of relationships is to look at individual identities – the vital centerpiece of coevolving relationships.

Harrison White and Frederic Godart (2003, p. 1) have contributed significantly to the understanding of social relationships from both social science and management perspectives. They enlarge on the idea that relationships are formed by a combination of self-organization, and the emergence and maintenance of individual personal identities.

They state that:

> An *identity* is triggered only out of efforts at *control* amid contingencies and contentions in interaction. Identities emerge from efforts at control in turbulent context. These control efforts need not have anything to do with coercion or domination over other identities. The root of control is finding footing in the biophysical and social environments. Such footing is a position that entails a stance, which brings orientation in relation to other identities. The control efforts by one identity are social realities for other identities. So an identity can be perceived by others as having an unproblematic continuity in social footing, even though it is adding through its contentions with others to the contingencies they face.

Social systems spontaneously self-organize into groups through the interactions individuals have with each other. These interactions create opportunities for each person to gain a stronger sense of their identity as individuals and in relation to other individuals, who are in turn also involved with gaining their own identity. Each person has an effect on others and is in return affected by others.

Thus, people need the freedom to explore and interact within their immediate environments to find their specific footing. Discovering what roles they can meaningfully assume in varying social settings, based on their talents and experiences, is another important effort.

With this in mind, you can begin to understand why so many people are disengaged at work. The rigid structures imposed on workplaces by top-down hierarchies and organizational charts restrict the free flow of emergent relationships. Many potentially beneficial relationships won't form because the barriers prevent opportunity. A person might never have the chance to discover strengths or overcome challenges if strict management parameters won't allow individual exploration. The natural networks that inevitably do come together do so only after overcoming the artificial barriers of authority and management.

Is it fair to ask how can a person be engaged when the work environment in many organizations seldom allows them to find their niche or maintain their personal identity? They most likely will find their niche external to the formal organization and thus remain relatively disengaged while at work.

To move toward an answer to that question let's take a closer look at relationships and identities from a complexity theory perspective.

Stacey, Griffin, and Shaw (2000, p. 123, 125) in *Complexity and Management* do a superb job of explaining how complexity theory needs to be used in managing our social institutions. They assert that:

> …an organization becomes what it is because of the intrinsic need human beings have, individually and collectively, to express their identities and thereby their differences. Identities and differences emerge, becoming what they are through the transformative cause of self-organization, that is, relationships. What an organization becomes emerges from the relationships of its members rather than being determined by the choices of individuals… Goals to do with competitive survival and profit are then seen to be subservient to this overriding need. This departs from dominant management views understanding performance as an all-important motivating force.

Notice the difference from the norm here: competitive survival and goals are subservient to the intrinsic human need to form relationships and express identities.

We can now begin to fully appreciate the power of relationships within organizations and extended networks. Stacey, Griffin, and Shaw make it quite clear why the need to express our identities overrides all other considerations including the profitability of an enterprise.

Sadly, as affirmed in *The Cluetrain Manifesto*, "Just about all the concessions we make to work in well-run, non-disturbing, secure, predictably successful, managed environments have to do with giving up our voice." Ironically, our voices and stories are the very underpinnings of our personal identities.

Another way of looking at the identity problem is that organizations and their functions are designed for the "average worker." This means an attempt to define everything from average intelligence, motivation, and skills to average personal goals, wages, and benefits.

Unfortunately, there is no such creature as an average person. So, until we find ways to provide workers the necessary personal freedom for identity expression and maintenance, even in relatively well-run organizations, the engagement gap will surely persist and most likely grow even wider.

Two Sides of Organizations

Now let's see how we can put to practical use what has been covered so far by exploring the duality of organizational constructs. Organizational life can typically be separated into two realms, or spheres of influence, as portrayed in Fig. 2.3: *management* and *unmanagement.*

The realm of management, depicted on the left, is an artificial entity usually devised by one or a handful of top executives of an enterprise. Management's aim is to control and "explicitly coordinate" the activities of people in the pursuit of organizational goals and objectives.

However, all life forms from amoebas to humans are self-organizing systems by design. That should immediately send up a red flag. Remember that organizational parameters can be adjusted, but that the behavior of people within those parameters can't be precisely predicted. The point of conflict is that people can be *influenced*, but not fully *controlled.*

As a result, unless the system is fully automated and people are completely eliminated from an organization, its members will seldom interact with one another exactly as management intends or prescribes.

The "unmanagement" realm depicted on the right is quite the opposite. Here emergent order and "implicit coordination" rule, since this side of the organization has no bosses or formal rules. What this means is that each member of the organization will

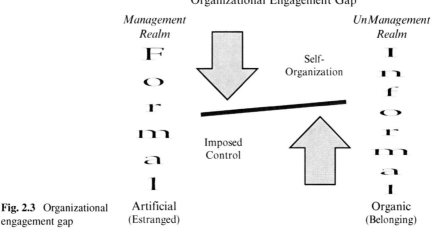

Fig. 2.3 Organizational engagement gap

interpret from his or her single perspective how best to work and survive within the parameters of their prescribed structure while keeping their identities intact.

If management attempts to meddle with an informal network in any way, the network will immediately morph into a different configuration to meet the challenge. Think of an amoeba changing shape to absorb food or to surround an intruding substance in its own defense.

In just about any organization, people will discuss their options with others and link up with members they believe have the same general ideas about how to prosper in their organization. They will take coping actions on their own if an unfamiliar or unexpected situation arises, and they'll do this with or without authorization from management. These "unauthorized" activities encompass both material and supervisory problems. You can count on them to happen since no artificially designed system can cover every contingency.

Simply put, that's how most of the work in organizations gets accomplished despite unforeseen events and management interventions. This also answers the question asked in Chap. 1: "How does any work get done at all?" It gets done by workers answering both the unofficial and the authorized calls to action through their own informal networks.

You also can begin to discern the primary "bonding factors" on each side of the organizational coin as seen in Fig. 2.3. On the management side, the emphasis is primarily on explicit coordination via official directives and policies. Transactions and conversations are generally formal, especially among administrators and employees. Acknowledged relationships are primarily confined to the circle of managers within the enterprise.

Conversely, on the side of "unmanagement," self-organization is the catalyst bringing about implicit coordination among the emergent networks situated both within and external to the organization. Transactions and conversations are mostly informal.

But notice that what really stands out on this side of the organization are the intimate and constantly evolving relationships. These relationships are the hidden assets that can make or break an enterprise. They are, of course, also affected by the organizational context within which people have to work. We will explore context in depth in Chap. 4.

The result on the formal "management" side of the organization is that "compliance" and "efficiency" receive primary attention in the pursuit of formal goals and objectives. Developing a sense of community is seldom addressed. Relationship is ignored.

On the contrary, members of the unmanagement realm thoroughly honor commitments made to fellow members of their own informal networks. A feeling of belonging and solidarity among the group members grows over time in varying degrees. People are committed to developing and maintaining their own and their compatriots' identities as best as possible.

Remember that "imposed control" does not trump "dynamic order." If management imposes more stringent, unwanted rules to try to control the members of an organization, then the informal networks will not disappear. Instead, they will become more fragmented and more clandestine in their activities. This, of course, can have some significantly detrimental effects for the enterprise if the emergent networks decide to undermine formal goals and activities.

The reverse is also true. The more employees are given a voice and implicit control in the management realm, the more they will understand and respond positively to formal organizational goals and initiatives. Also in the process, the informal networks will begin to function more in the open and start making appropriate connections with other emergent groups. They will begin to overlap with other groups, as well as with management.

This overlap is a very desirable state where the formal system and the informal networks both agree with the overall organizational goals and processes. The agreement doesn't come through formal negotiations. It is a natural outgrowth of day-to-day interactions, or circular causality.

I have labeled this place of common agreement as the "shared-access domain," shown in Fig. 2.4. This overlapping area is the optimal organizational "sweet spot."

It's important to remember that the two systems don't merge and become one, even though members of both the formal and informal camps participate. Instead, in the shared-access domain, implicit coordination based on circular causality is the predominant operating mode.

Ideally, the two spheres should overlap completely making the entire organization the shared-access domain. In reality, a complete overlap is not possible, even in smaller organizations of fewer than 150 members for two reasons.

First, all organizations, large or small, need some type of a formally recognized framework for internal and especially external communications to effectively coordinate their overall activities.

These communication frameworks don't need to be hierarchical or linear. All that's needed is for everyone involved to understand and adhere to agreed-upon communications rules. The bottom line is that all ventures need uniformly recognized policies and procedures to facilitate effective transactions and conversations.

This is why the formal side of an organization can never be entirely abolished, and therefore because of its nature, never wholly incorporated into the shared-access domain.

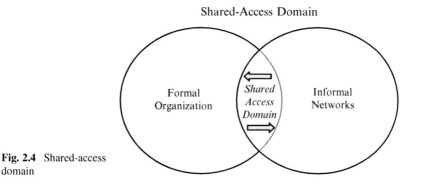

Fig. 2.4 Shared-access domain

Of course, when possible, it's best to encourage and facilitate face-to-face interactions since they better promote codependent long-term relationships. Organizations or subdivisions within organizations that have memberships of fewer than 150 command the advantage in this respect, since face-to-face interactions are more feasible in smaller groups. I'll elaborate on the implications of group size more extensively in Chap. 6.

Second, every organization, whether it's a book club or a city government, has an informal social system of various emergent networks. However, it is also true that not all informal network members will choose to participate in the shared-access domain activities all the time. This means that at any given moment there will always be some members on the informal side of a venture who are outside the sweet spot.

By taking another look at Fig. 2.4, we can now begin to visualize why the formal and informal circles can never fully overlap. The part of the formal organizational which holds all the operationally needed rules and procedures will always remain outside the shared-access domain (to the left in the figure). No matter how flexible or accommodating the organization may be, the formal framework simply can't be completely incorporated into the completely self-organizing shared-access domain.

Similarly, a part of the informal organizational will also linger outside and to the right of the shared-access domain as depicted in Fig. 2.4. That is, no matter how supportive a venture's social context may be in facilitating self-organization throughout an enterprise, not all emergent network members will choose to participate in the productive activities of the sweet spot.

A certain number of people will always be disengaged from work, busying themselves with such things as honing mutually supportive relationships, establishing a firm footing for their identities, or simply having a bad day. That, of course, prevents the entire informal side of an organization from being totally incorporated into the shared-access domain.

Another vital difference among the three domains is the underlying priorities. It's helpful to keep these points in mind when examining the dynamics surrounding the shared-access domain:

- On the formal side, strictly controlling all activities and increasing profitability reigns supreme.
- In the shared-access domain, self-organization that creates "dynamic order" in support of organizational goals reigns supreme.
- On the informal side, self-organization dominates the scene, but not necessarily in support of organizational goals. Considerable time and effort is also devoted to developing codependent relationships and maintaining individual identities.

In the simplest terms, just remember these three primary factors and their specific attributes influencing the activities of the shared-access domain:

- The formal system equates to control and profits.
- The shared-access domain equates to productive dynamic order.
- The informal networks equate to relationships and identities.

What stands out above is that only the formal system can be "managed." Neither the shared-access domain nor the informal networks can be managed because they are "emergent." They can, however, be influenced. Hence, the formal system needs to be constantly "fine tuned" not just by management alone, but also with the involvement of all members of an organization to expand the shared-access domain.

Why? Because the sweet spot is where most of the productive work and innovation takes place in an enterprise. That will become progressively clearer in the chapters that follow.

Research by Scanlan has demonstrated that some individuals can work only at 20–30% of their ability and still retain their jobs. I suggest they retain their positions by making sure that they only follow official directives and policies as much as "visibility necessitates" yet ignore most everything else at work that may need their attention.

So, is there any question why most of the interest in every enterprise should be mainly focused on the organizational sweet spot? As one can see it's precisely there where roughly 60–80% of the work and innovation takes place. Unfortunately, most organizations are still more concerned with saving money by streamlining transactions, keeping conversations to the bare minimum, and ignoring or even trying to eliminate relationships. How smart is that?

Main Considerations

As we have just seen, it is possible for management and unmanagement to merge extensively in the shared-access domain to the benefit of the entire enterprise. From this new perspective, we should leave behind the old mechanistic general systems theory and the automated control systems, or cybernetics, still widely used today. Instead we should turn a keen eye to the forward-looking theory of complex adaptive systems that describes self-organizing systems.

The reason is straight forward: general systems theory and cybernetics are deterministic while human actions are not. The complex adaptive systems theory framework, on the contrary, places emphasis on self-organization as the driving force in the emergent transformative interactions among individuals, within networks, and between multiple networks. As Stacey, Griffin, and Shaw (2000, p. 123–124) conclude:

> This puts cooperative interaction, or relationship, and the conflicting constraints that relationship imposes, right at the center of the creative process of organizational development. Since power is constraint, this perspective places power, politics and conflict at the center of the cooperative social process through which joint action is taken. Novel organizational developments are caused by the political, social and psychological nature of human relations. This departs from the dominant discourse of management in which the role of the manager is one of removing ambiguity and conflict to secure consensus.

Ironically, this is precisely how we modern humans managed to survive quite nicely for the first 200,000 years of our existence.

We should also keep in mind several tenets as we try to develop more vibrant and creative transformative organizations and networks. Let's look at the six main tenets:

1. Unavoidability of unmanagement
2. Freedom of association (autonomy)
3. Individual and group responsibilities
4. Unpredictability and goal flexibility
5. Evolutionary psychology and neuroscience or human nature
6. Catalytic leadership

Unavoidability of Unmanagement

First, one should never forget that the unmanagement or informal side of an organization will always be present. The other cardinal rule is that these emergent networks can't be managed or controlled.

For dramatic proof, talk to a survivor of a gulag or concentration camp about how they stayed alive, or find a good book about it. Prisoners will tell you the same thing. You will quickly discover that their survival was mostly dependent on the ingenuity of the spontaneous networks that sprang up among the prisoners within those horrendous places. They conducted their survival operations right under the noses of guards manning machine guns in watch towers and patrolling the fence lines with attack dogs.

So, administrators of every organization must make a clear choice. Do they want to push the informal networks underground or allow them to function openly for the benefit of the entire organization?

The second option is obviously better because you will seldom know whether the underground folks are working with you or against you. It's pretty tough to run a successful enterprise when a bunch of folks are disengaged and are using their ingenuity to undermine day-to-day operations. That energy and resourcefulness can and should be put to much more productive use.

Freedom of Association (Autonomy)

Personal freedom and autonomy are important factors in the pursuit and maintenance of one's identity. It is also vital for creativity. How else can a person or a team within an organization establish meaningful relationships or create a virtuous cycle of innovation in the quest for new processes, products, and services without autonomy?

For example, an individual should have the freedom to voluntarily join several teams as long as all the work commitments are satisfactorily honored. The old saying, "You should give up control to gain control," is a good maxim for management to follow.

The upshot is that it's impossible to fully control human behavior other than by physically restraining someone. There is no way to get into someone's head to foretell personal intentions, choices to be made, or the actions he or she will take. Hence, personal freedom and self-organization are the best options, especially when you have the right people assembled.

Individual and Group Responsibilities

As a general rule, temper freedom with responsibility. People who want to be members of a Transformational Organization must demonstrate their willingness to take full responsibility, not only for their own actions but also for the actions or inactions of the organization as a whole.

A free-flowing self-organizing institution or network has no traditional managers to give directives. Therefore, every network member takes responsibility for actively assuring that agreed-upon goals are met and potential problems and opportunities are brought to everyone's attention. Thus, part of the social responsibility includes assuming "catalytic" leadership (fully defined in Chap. 5) roles when an opportunity presents itself. Free riders have short life spans in an open self-organizing system.

Unpredictability and Goal Flexibility

As mentioned previously, no system can be designed to meet all possible contingencies. Standard statistical routines can only be realistically applied to known historical data (looking in the rear view mirror) and are of little value in predicting truly novel random events or "Black Swans," a term coined by Nassim Nicholas Taleb.

Our goals and associated plans should be focused on the short-range to mid-range time span (2–5 years out). Goals and plans are certainly an important part of running any organization, but they should be flexible and constantly updated to depict the current realistic environmental conditions. Given that the emergence of completely new relationship patterns creates novelty, developing a grand vision or detailed strategic plan for the next 10 to 20 years is comparable to writing a fairytale.

Prescriptive advice such as benchmarks to social systems should be applied carefully. Benchmarks are dated concepts that may have helped one or a handful of organizations to succeed in certain areas. That's fine as long as we remember that every social network has its own unique qualities and chemistry that is impossible to precisely duplicate.

For best results, a creative free flowing organization should function somewhere near the top of the complexity arc or the edge of chaos, as suggested by Jeffrey Kluger in *Simplexity*. That means working someplace between complete disorder and order. That, of course, is a judgment call.

Evolutionary Psychology or Human Nature

Our evolved predispositions are important from the standpoint of our innate behavioral tendencies. Humans are not born a blank slate. Instead, we arrive with all the basic rudiments of our mental circuitry in place, ready to act in response to our immediate environment. At the same time, we are able to learn from our experiences, molding our capabilities into practical capacities even as infants.

Thus, humans are equipped not only with instincts, but also with much broader innate drives or capabilities, such as concern for status and for affiliation. This means that our behavior is influenced by our genes and neural networks rather than genetically determined. We do have free will.

Human nature carries with it a number of implications about how we think, form relationships, behave in small and large groups, and about our preferences for particular organizational frameworks. We need to pay attention to these vital issues when dealing with relationship and emergent networks. Admittedly, having least a working knowledge of evolutionary psychology and social neuroscience helps.

Catalytic Leadership

Transformational Organizations should practice "catalytic" or nonbossing leadership. Chapter 5 is entirely devoted to leadership, so suffice it to say here that catalytic leadership has nothing in common with traditional hierarchical position power. Catalytic leadership, as I have defined it, is "encouraging others to participate in value-added activities that they are either not aware of or are hesitant to initiate on their own that would benefit everyone involved." It's essentially all about bringing people and ideas together and sorting out the most meaningful possibilities for mutually beneficial action.

The six main considerations briefly discussed above will, to one degree or another, receive further attention and clarification in the remainder of the chapters.

In the next chapter, we'll identify and discuss the most important relationship factors and their impact on individual identity and creativity.

References

Kluger, J. (2008) *Simplexity: How Simple Things Become Complex*. New York: Hyperion.
Levine, F., Locke, C., Searls, D. and Weinberger, D. (2000) *The Cluetrain Manifesto: The End of Business as Usual*. Cambridge, MA: Perseus.
Scanlan, B. K. (1981) "Creating a Climate for Achievement." *Business Horizons*, March–April, pp. 5–9.

Stacey, R. D., Griffin, D. and Shaw, P. (2000) *Complexity and Management: Fad or Radical Challenge to Systems Thinking?* New York: Routledge.

Stevens, A. and Price, T. (1996) *Evolutionary Psychiatry: A New Beginning.* New York: Routledge.

Taleb, N. N. (2007) *The Black Swan: The Impact of the Highly Improbable.* New York: Random House.

White, H. C. and Godart, F. C. (2003) "Stories from Identity and Control." *Sociologica*, March, Nr. 3, pp. 1–17, 10.2383/25960.

Chapter 3
Relationship and Identity Development

So far we've covered transformational relationships in general terms. Discovering and understanding the intricately and dynamically interrelated features of relationships, however, requires a much deeper investigation.

The three basic factors of transformational relationships are (1) evolved human predispositions, (2) tacit knowledge, and (3) social capital. These features, which we'll call the "triad" for simplicity, have some intriguing attributes.

First, these factors are essential to life success. They will evolve in a person in a specific way in response to differing biophysical and social contexts. In technical terms, they are life sustaining and nondeterministic.

Second, they are unpredictable and limitless from an individual's behavioral perspective.

Third, related closely to the first two points, is that they are not controllable. Because human predisposition, tacit knowledge, and social capital are not tangible, they cannot be managed by anyone to bring about specific outcomes. These three factors are the basis for the intrinsic, emergent, and receptive processes of coevolving relationships. Therefore, in this chapter we will focus on one fundamental social process and the three key relationship factors listed above.

The deep-seated process governing the activities of all living entities is self-organization or circular causality. Keep in mind that each individual factor of the triad functions in accordance with the dynamics of circular causality – they affect and are affected by each other.

In essence, we will be dealing with an integrated framework created by multiple interacting self-organizing entities that form and sustain individual and organizational identities.

Self-Organization/Circular Causality

All people and social institutions constantly self-organize to adapt to the ever shifting conditions of their immediate surroundings. Self-organization begins at the molecular level in individuals as each biological system of our human physical

C. Ehin, *The Organizational Sweet Spot: Engaging the Innovative Dynamics of Your Social Networks*,
DOI 10.1007/978-0-387-98194-9_3, © Springer Science+Business Media, LLC 2009

body works to keep us healthy and functioning optimally in our physical world. This self-organization extends from internal processes to an individual's contact with the external environment.

Individual Self-Organization

Let's look at the self-organization process that happens within our own physical system – the human body. It applies to the interaction of trillions of cells in our bodies and the billions of neurons of our brains. The entire system organizes itself constantly, assuring that the mind and body function maximally at any given moment.

Circular causality (explained in Chap. 2) is at work here as well. That is, systems A, B, and C affect each other simultaneously in a circular fashion rather than in a step-by-step cause-and-effect linear fashion.

Each human body is a network of interdependent systems that create, repair, destroy, and eliminate millions of cells constantly to keep our corporal selves operating at top efficiency and effectiveness at all times.

Not only that, our physical organic systems of respiration, blood circulation, skin, endocrine, nerves, bone, and digestion all affect each other in a complex and dynamic way to achieve optimal bodily functions. The wonder of it all is that there is no specific agent within the human physical system doing the organizing. It just happens.

In short, each physical being self-organizes to survive and thrive as individuals. If that were not the case we could not survive for a second. More specifically, as Camazine et al. (2003, p. 8) point out:

> In biological systems self-organization is a process in which patterns at the global level of a system emerge solely from numerous interactions among the lower-level components of the system. Moreover, the rules specifying interactions among the system's components are executed using only local information, without reference to the global pattern.

In essence, human survival is an uncontrollable process. We should keep that in mind in developing our organizational contexts.

Social Self-Organization

This process is also at work externally and is present whenever people interact with their social environments. When someone comes in contact with other individuals and groups, he or she reacts and interacts with them in a way appropriate to the situation. These interactions change in a complex and dynamic way as we create, repair, destroy, and eliminate social relationships to solve a common problem or take advantage of a specific opportunity.

Fig. 3.1 Visualizing self-organization

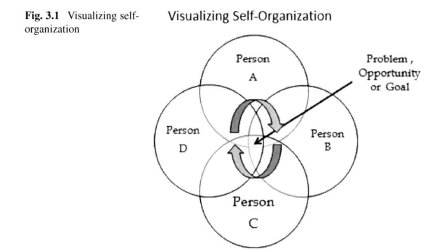

Circular causality is again in play as individuals and groups affect others and are, in turn, affected by others. As with our bodily systems, individuals self-organize in social groups within their environments to survive and thrive in society.

So we begin to see that self-organization takes place at all levels through the process of circular causality.

Figure 3.1 is a visual portrayal of the self-organization process. The depicted dynamics in this case apply to the interactions of several people revolving around a common goal or problem to solve. This process is relevant whether we're investigating the interrelationships among cells, small groups, organizations, or multiple networks.

The interactions depicted here are mutually reinforcing and usually intensify over time when perpetuated by a common goal or problem. Clearly, circular causality or self-organization is a never-ending process and continues as new people join or drop out of an endeavor.

Therefore, the focus of our social institutions should be on developing dynamic frameworks that support the self-organizing processes of its emergent networks openly instead of trying to suppress or control the behavior of people.

Here is a synopsis of the most important points about self-organization:

- It's an entity's intrinsic ability to change itself as it interacts with its environment and strives to maintain its identity.
- Interactions produce self-referential patterns without the need to be designed or managed.
- Evolving patterns are both sustained and transformed by spontaneous interactions.
- Creativity and destruction are part of the emergent process.
- All life forms are self-organizing systems by design.

Our Evolved Predispositions

In our development as modern humans, we inherited not only our physical but also our mental attributes from our hunter-gatherer ancestors. The genetic development of primitive humans was in direct response to the need and conditions of that time.

Life forms generally evolve to cope with specific, immediate environmental conditions. Since the evolutionary process doesn't anticipate the future, it never wastes vital resources on giving an organism a capacity that it can't use immediately.

It's important to realize that the genetic predispositions, or innate drives, of modern humans evolved eons ago to help us cope with the needs and conditions of small hunter-gatherer societies on the African Savannah, long before the human migration to other continents. Essentially, our behavior evolved first and the ability to make sense of it developed later.

Our genetic tendencies are the very foundation of how we interact with one another. Namely, they are the core of the continuous self-organizing process that takes place as we get together with other individuals and groups. As Professor Nigel Nicholson (2008, p. 74) of the London Business School suggests, "This has a number of ramifications in how we think and feel, the form and process of social relationships, our behavior in groups, our responses to symbols, and our preferences for certain institutional forms."

Our evolved capabilities aren't just purely instinctive. They cover a much broader and much more flexible range of behaviors, including drives. For example, we blink when something unexpectedly flashes by our eyes, or we jump when a loud noise startles us. These are instinctive reactions and are more or less automatic in response to certain stimuli. Instincts direct our responses.

Innate drives are much less automatic; we have much more leeway in how we respond. For instance, we all crave fatty, sweet, and salty foods. The difference is that we have free will to override those yearnings. These are genetic predispositions that nudge rather than direct us to behave in a certain way, but they are not fully instinctive. Recent studies also suggest that such behavioral factors as conscientiousness, happiness, and morality have a genetic foundation.

Therefore, it shouldn't be a big surprise to anyone how people decide whether they like or dislike someone new the moment they shake a stranger's hand and say, "hello." It's partially genetic.

Researchers have concluded that about 50% of an individual's potential for behavior is inherited, including the potential for happiness and morality. We are all born with certain "base line" inherited predispositions or *set points*. These set points are also referred to as *ultimate causes* and are the reason an individual's personality doesn't fluctuate much over a life span.

The good news is that there is quite a range of potential behaviors that are not genetic set points. The other 50%, or *proximate causes*, play out through life experiences.

What this means, for example, is that if you were born as a relatively reserved individual you will never be a real party animal. However, that doesn't mean you can't work to increase your sociability, especially if that means doing so will make you happier. We have the ability to shift that behavior trait within our normal range, when a desire motivates us to change. In time and with practice, the new behavior becomes more habitual and more practical. The increased sociability becomes an evolved capability.

It is also true of all our other talents and capabilities. The more we use them the more proficient we become. Essentially, through application and experience, we expand our evolved capabilities into practical capacities.

So, what are some of our foremost inherited predispositions or innate drives? Innate drives seem to come in roughly two major categories. Multiple authors have given these categories different names. For our purposes, we'll call them *self-centered*, for drives such as concern for control, rank, status, territory, possessions, and violence, and *other-centered* for drives such as concern for attachments, affiliation, altruism, care giving, care receiving, morality, and empathy.

People seem to function best in a constructive social context where both self- and other-centered drives can be freely expressed in a balanced manner. Such an environment would have individuals who willingly express a mix of both moderate self-interest and outward-reaching altruism. This type of social context promotes implicit coordination and is also vital for sharing tacit knowledge, which is explained next.

It's also important to remember that, in general, there isn't one particular gene for every predisposition. For instance, no specific gene exists for concern with attachment or domination. Our bodies are parallel operating systems where every component works together simultaneously. Thus, all of our genes, cells, and neurons work in concert with one another. Some genes may have a more dominant role than others in certain behaviors, but usually none plays an all-inclusive part.

Further, our evolved capabilities have little to do with genetic determinism. Rather, as Colin Tudge (2000, p. 154) makes clear:

> …we should be prepared to use our brains to override 'nature.' We should seek to ensure that our brains…are the ultimate arbiters. But we should not underestimate nature. Our inherited nature *includes* much of what any of us would call morality; it *includes* a respect for fellow creatures. So although we might override nature, we would do well to listen to nature too. We all know what 'conscience' is: the 'inner voice' that tells us we are behaving badly. We need not doubt that that 'inner voice' is itself evolved, calling to us from our difficult days on the African plains.

Understanding that 50% of our behavior is genetically based helps us in five general ways.

First, knowing that we are born with two archetypical behavioral modes allows us to at least partially anticipate the needs and behavior of people under various environmental conditions.

For instance, people immersed in a very competitive, position, power, and compliance-oriented organization will behave and think in a correspondingly defensive way no matter what they say in public or what is formally requested. Asking people to be good team players in such a context is foolish. Such an achievement is impossible unless the company's facilities catch on fire and even then it may be doubtful.

Second, no two individuals can respond exactly the same way to a particular problem or opportunity no matter how closely their genetic behavioral set points match.

As an example, people who find themselves in the competitive organization described above will express their anger differently. Some with a relatively high predisposition for anger will most likely express their frustrations more often and more vehemently. Others will be more restrained, even when they are at the very high end of their anger set point. Within the full range of anger reactions, no two people will express it exactly the same way because their genetic makeup is different.

Third, fully grasping the duality of our evolved dispositions allows us to design organizational ecologies that enhance rather than hinder relationship development.

Even when we choose to operate some of our social institutions in a very compliance-oriented top-down style, we need to be aware of the negative impact such a restrictive environment has on our inherent predispositions. Why, for instance, does the average employee only work at two-thirds of his or her capacity? Why is worker loyalty so low? Why is almost 20% of the US workforce totally disengaged?

These questions need to be answered with actual solutions, not better slogans. We will take a closer look at some solutions to these problems in the next three chapters.

Fourth, it is essential to realize that our innate drives can't be circumvented. They are operating at all times no matter what kind of a setting we find ourselves in.

Yes, there is a range on either side of the genetic set points, but beyond that range the drives can't be manipulated. Again, we can change organizational settings but we can't fully predict or control human behavior.

That's why, for example, the movie producers, advertising agencies, and the media generally focus on sex and violence. These subjects impact our most basic self-centered predispositions that evolved hundreds of millions of years ago and which are most easily activated. Our other-centered drives, which developed much later, take more effort to be fully expressed.

Fifth, humans function best in an environment where both the self-centered and the other-centered dispositions have a chance to be expressed. Fostering both sides of human nature is a vital success factor for our kind.

Neuroscientists Berntson and Cacioppo stipulate that a fundamental innate computation carried out by humans is the differentiation between hostile and hospitable stimuli. Obviously it's a vital survival computation that allows us to adapt our behavior according to the situation.

In other words, we figure out if a situation is hostile or helpful and react accordingly. The reactions are either self – or other-centered depending on how we read each situation. Learning to recognize and balance the two as integral parts of our being allows us to work within groups and gives us the best opportunity to meet our individual *and social demands.*

Dual Brain Functions

We humans tend to ignore or forget our evolutionary past, even though we have not only much in common with our most recent cousins, the primates, but also with reptiles whose ancestry goes back more than 400 million years. For discussion purposes, the brain is regarded in three main levels: hindbrain, mid-brain (limbic system), and frontal brain (cerebral cortex).

We inherited the lowest level of our brains, the hindbrain, from the reptiles which is mostly governed by instincts where the primary focus is on self-preservation. This level of brain function explains why it's still so easy for people to kill other people when confronted by certain circumstances.

We inherited our mid-brain, or limbic system, from other mammals. The well-known evolutionary biologist Edward O. Wilson (1998, p. 107) calls it "the master traffic-control complex that regulates emotional responses as well as the integration and transfer of sensory information." This includes major emotions such as fear, anger, love, and attachment.

Lastly, the cerebral cortex gives us our most human qualities of perceptual categorization, memory and learning, and language. In most mammals the cerebral cortex accounts for about 35% of total brain volume, while in primates it varies from a low of 50% in some monkeys to roughly 80% in humans. According to Dunbar, the human neocortex, which is another name for the cerebral cortex, is larger than those of other primates mainly because of our increased social complexity.

What's most pertinent here is that all three levels of our brains work together in a self-organizing manner. Therefore, we seldom are aware which level is on stage at a given time. As evolutionary psychiatrist Kent Bailey has said, the hindbrain is "where free will steps aside and persons act as they have to act, often despising themselves in the process for their hatreds, prejudices, compulsions, conformity, deceptiveness, and guile."

So, thanks to all three levels of our brain, humans can be the most compassionate or the most vicious animals in the world, depending on the circumstances they find themselves in and how they got there, and upon which level of the brain is responding at that moment.

I believe the duality of human nature can be illustrated best by an example. The Cherokee legend below vividly demonstrates the continuous interplay of our self- and other-centered genetic predispositions as we respond to different biophysical and social environmental contexts:

> An old Cherokee is teaching his grandson about life. "A fight is going on inside me," he said to the boy.
>
> It is a terrible fight and it is between two wolves. One is evil – he is anger, envy, sorrow, regret, greed, arrogance, self-pity, guilt, resentment, inferiority – lies, false pride, superiority, and ego. "He continued," The other is good – he is joy, peace, love, hope, serenity, humility, kindness, benevolence, empathy, generosity, truth, compassion, and faith.
>
> The same fight is going on inside you - and inside every other person, too."

The grandson thought about it for a minute and then asked his grandfather,
"Which wolf will win?"
The old Cherokee simply replied, "The one you feed."

Perception is the key factor in determining which "wolf" we select to feed.
That is, how we read a particular situation determines whether we need to look out
primarily for the welfare of ourselves, or also for the people in our sphere of
influence. That's why organizational contexts are so important in influencing our
behavior. We'll explore this point in more detail in the next chapter.

Hormones and Brain Cell Types and the Roles They Play

Several more key points about human nature need to be clarified. Humans come
outfitted with hormones that explicitly promote trust and bonding. They are oxy-
tocin and vasopressin. According to psychologist Edward Hallowell (1999, p. 63):

> ...these hormones are always present to some degree in all of us, but they rise when we feel
> empathy for another person—in particular when we are meeting with someone face-to-face.
> It has been shown that these bonding hormones are at suppressed levels when people are
> physically separate, which is one of the reasons that it is easier to deal harshly with someone
> via e-mail than in person. Furthermore, scientists hypothesize that in person contact
> stimulates two important neurotransmitters: dopamine, which enhances attention and
> serotonin, which reduces fear and worry.

In the past 5 years, social neuroscience has made significant strides in identifying
parts of our brain circuitry directly related to behavior and motivation. For example,
recently discovered "mirror" brain cells mimic the behavior of people we come in
direct physical contact with. This innate process allows us to emulate the emotions
of people we're around, creating an instantaneous shared experience of fun or
gloom. In addition, as Goleman and Boyatzis (2008, p. 77) explain:

> Intuition, too, is in the brain, produced in part by a class of neurons called *spindle cells*
> because of their shape...Spindle cells trigger neural networks that come into play whenever
> we have to choose the best response among many...These cells also help us gauge whether
> someone is trustworthy and right (or wrong) for the job. Within one-twentieth of a second,
> our spindle cells fire with information about how we feel about that person; such "thin-slice"
> judgments can be very accurate, as follow-up metrics reveal.

In addition, "oscillator" neurons "coordinate people physically by regulating how
and when their bodies move together." Ever try feigning a real hug? The phoniness
is instantly recognizable.

What this suggests is that when direct face-to-face interaction is lacking, totally
virtual organizations and networks are unable to develop the close relationships and
trust among people that is required for high levels of social engagement. Hence, at
least periodic face-to-face meetings among people need to happen for elevated
levels of trust to develop and more progressive innovation dynamics to develop.

During the course of evolution, the human mind didn't give up instincts but
instead expanded them in becoming more adept in dealing with social complexity.

Thus, each person decides appropriate behavior based on a combination of both evolved predispositions and life experiences. They are the internal criteria that guide us to take certain kinds of action or to ignore others as we continuously scan and categorize the activities around us.

Human behavior isn't just the function of deterministic genetic processes. Instead, our behavior is very complex, nonlinear, and quite unpredictable.

I suggest that as we plan organizational structures, we keep in mind these facts about our evolved predispositions:

- Human behavior is based on a complex relationship between nature and nurture. None of us are either physically or mentally exactly alike.
- Our self-centered capabilities/predispositions, in general, consist of concern for control, status, territory, possessions, envy, vengeance, etc.
- Our other-centered capabilities/predispositions, in general, consist of concern for attachment, affiliation, altruism, care-giving/receiving, morality, empathy, etc.
- Productive relationships typically develop in social contexts where group size is limited to about 150 codependent people allowing people to freely express a mix of moderate self-interest and outward-reaching altruism. Explained in more detail in Chap. 6.
- True relationships require codependent face-to-face interactions. Without in-person interfaces our hormones; neurotransmitters; and mirror, spindle, and oscillators brain cell have little chance of being fully engaged limiting meaningful social engagement.

Tacit Knowledge

Scientist and philosopher Michael Polanyi is given credit for the concept of tacit knowledge. In *Personal Knowledge*, Polanyi suggests that personalized knowledge is fundamentally the tacit integration of all we have observed and learned which we then use to respond to differing environmental contexts and situations. Polanyi essentially used the term to describe a process rather than a form of knowledge as it's mostly used today. Above all, as we'll see in the next chapter, tacit knowledge is a critical commodity in the innovation process.

Tacit knowledge is the compilation of an individual's world view that is founded primarily on personal experiences rather than formal education. That suggests that tacit knowledge is acquired through first-hand experiences and interactions with more knowledgeable people and groups rather than through books or seminars.

For example, future architects typically earn a degree at an accredited university where they are introduced to a body of formal or explicit knowledge. But that isn't enough for a person to become an effective architect. Architectural firms usually require new employees to acquire experience (tacit knowledge) through some sort of on the job training or apprenticeship before they can be considered proficient enough to work independently.

Tacit knowledge, because it is unrelated to specific facts and events, can't be found in databases, documents, books, files, libraries, or the Internet. It can only be partially shared orally and it can't be codified or transmitted by formal means since nobody is fully aware of all the disparate knowledge that they possess. Tacit knowledge, therefore, includes ideas and generalizations at the individual level.

Also, tacit knowledge must be allowed to emerge. It can't be forced or supervised out of people.

We also know today that many of the neural memory networks involved in acquiring tacit knowledge (or implicit learning as it is termed below) have evolved separately from what is accessible by the conscious brain. According to neuroscientist Joseph LeDoux (2002, p. 117):

> Each of us has his or her own style of walking, talking, and thinking…We notice things that some others ignore, and ignore things that some people notice…The extent to which we are calm and collected, or emotionally reactive, when things go awry…as are the logical paths and illogical leaps of thought we have. These and many other aspects of mind and behavior are expressed so automatically, so implicitly, that they may be unchangeable, perhaps innate. But we should not overlook the crucial role of experience, which is to say of learning and memory, in establishing and maintaining them.

Tacit knowledge is so fundamental and makes our daily routines so automatic; we wouldn't survive a day without it. Can you imagine having to think through every task you undertake, step by step, from start to finish including getting out of bed, brushing your teeth, riding a bicycle, or writing an e-mail? Without this repertoire of unconnected know-how, we wouldn't be able to suitably categorize people, places, and events instantaneously so we could take appropriate action when we encounter them.

We are all continuously exposed to all sorts of values, facts, perceptions, and events from the first to the last day of our journey on earth. This journey of experiences combined with our evolved capabilities is how we develop our "worldview" based on our experiences, assumptions, perceptions, values, fears, and so on. Because the nature of each person's worldview is so deeply embedded and automatic, we can never completely access and articulate our worldview.

In the same way, it's not possible to directly transfer our tacit knowledge to other people and groups by such means as seminars, and training manuals. For example, when was the last time anyone learned to ride a bicycle by reading an instruction manual? We all know that the only way to learn to ride a bike is to get on one and experience what it takes to stay on it. You can show someone or coach them, but you can't put the experience into another person's head without them actually trying it. That's tacit knowledge.

Further, every person is similar in a general way to other human beings in that we all have similar basic physical and mental characteristics. But we are quite different from one another in our appearance as well as our cognitive capabilities. What this means is that each individual acquires expertise in his or her own unique way and applies it in a distinctive fashion. Therefore, tacit knowledge is a very dynamic and pliable resource. Its acquisition and use is an emergent process that can be influenced, but not managed.

Fig. 3.2 Tacit knowledge
dynamics

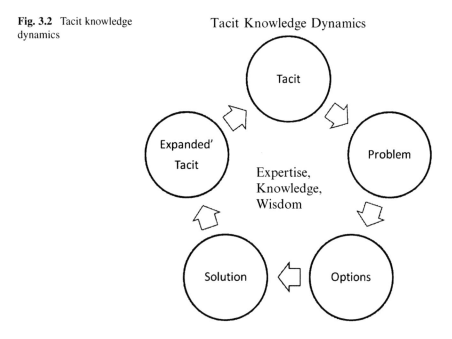

Tacit Knowledge Dynamics

Moreover, it's important to keep in mind that the wellspring of all new codified or explicit knowledge is tacit knowledge. For instance, tacit knowledge usually comes to the fore when people try to solve newly encountered problems or take advantage of new opportunities. Tacit knowledge derives its potency from the fact that it is instantly accessible, practical, and malleable given the right circumstances. It is the starting point for new discoveries.

Figure 3.2 illustrates the fundamental dynamics of tacit knowledge in facilitating the development of new explicit and tacit knowledge. Let's suppose an individual encounters a problem that they haven't come across previously. Starting at the first step (top of the figure), that person immediately tries to solve the problem by trying to recall similar predicaments in the past and solutions or a combination of solutions (tacit knowledge) that may apply to the present situation (problem).

If that's not sufficient, the person may then do some additional research or consult with someone who has some expertise with similar events. Eventually the problem is solved (solution) with some very precise (explicit) procedures and if necessary appropriate parts or materials. A key point to remember in developing new innovative processes or procedures is that tacit knowledge must be first made explicit before it can be properly applied.

Finally, the dynamic process in turn would have made additional contributions to the tacit knowledge of the individual or individuals participating in solving the novel problem. As one can see, the use and expansion of tacit knowledge is a continuous virtuous cycle that never ends unless an individual run out of problems to solve or opportunities to pursue. That, of course, seldom happens in real life.

Does tacit knowledge have a down side? Yes, it does. Some people accumulate all sorts of strange facts, values, assumptions, and ideas in the course of their lives. As a result, when they reach into their "bag of tacit tricks" what emerges may be unique, but quite useless.

The catch and the big issue in today's work environment is that for tacit knowledge to properly emerge and be useful for problem solving, people must first be surrounded by a supportive environment. Threats, for example, create negative emotions that, by necessity, narrow thought patterns. People threatened by the loss of their jobs, a bullying boss, unreasonable deadlines, and so on, innately narrow their thought patterns to avoid or eliminate these negative emotions.

As a result, individuals in such circumstances devote little or no time engaging their minds more expansively and resourcefully in search of new ideas or opportunities. Tacit knowledge is rendered dormant because of the threat or suppression experienced at work. All incentives for sharing knowledge are lost. People disengage.

For the US workforce, that's about 24.7 million workers who are actively disengaged from their jobs.

Thus, it makes considerable sense for organizations and networks to develop social contexts where tacit knowledge is welcomed and where collaborative relationships are nurtured.

In summary, here are the main characteristics of tacit knowledge:

- Consists of uncodified knowledge (grounded in both genes and experience) that people carry in their minds that is difficult to access or share.
- Effective transfer normally requires extensive personal contact and trust.
- Composed of habits and culture that we do not recognize in ourselves.
- Different areas of the brain are involved in accessing tacit and explicit memory.
- Is the wellspring of new codified or explicit knowledge.

Social Capital

Social capital generally refers to the informal relationships between individuals, and within and between emergent social networks. As the term implies, these evolving networks have value for the people associated or immersed within them.

Adler and Seok-Woo's (2002, p. 23) definition of social capital is most useful. They say that, "Social capital is the goodwill available to individuals or groups. Its source lies in the structure and content of the actor's social relations. Its effects flow from the information, influence, and solidarity it makes available to the actor [or actors]."

Fundamentally, social capital is our inherent inclination to engage in mutually beneficial social activities for the benefit of all concerned.

Unlike other forms of capital, social capital is owned mutually by the members of a given network. It can't be traded or sold like other assets, and no single party has exclusive rights to it. Also, social capital increases in value the more it's used rather than being depleted like financial resources.

Social capital is also not the same as human capital. Human capital actually is an economic commodity, but social capital is an intrinsic, emergent, and receptive process based on mutually beneficial relationships.

In essence, social capital is based on the trusting and mutual relationships formed by people over time. It is composed of tight-knit support networks that provide the information, influential connections, and camaraderie needed by all of us for meaningful existence. It's an intangible that can't be managed or controlled.

Social capital is the very foundation of voluntary interdependent associations. It develops through circular causality as opposed to top-down directives and executive power. You can also call it a network of coevolved relationships.

We're all quite aware that few things in organizations are accomplished by strictly following formal directives. Without enough social capital, an enterprise is merely a collection of employees or hired hands, incapable of taking action on their own, always waiting for instructions from bosses.

Sit back for a moment and reflect how you carry out your responsibilities at work. Do you follow all policies and directives to the letter? You probably do that just enough to stay out of trouble. Further, when you encounter something novel, do you immediately run to your boss for advice, or do you improvise to solve the problem with the help of your associates?

Is it any wonder that roughly 70% of work gets accomplished informally?

Further, Putnam and Feldstein discuss the duality of social capital and distinguish between "bonding" and "bridging" social capital. Bonding networks are very close knit entities composed of like-minded people. They are inward looking and generally don't view outsiders kindly. Bridging social networks, however, are more diverse and outward looking. Consequently, they are more likely to link up with other informal groups in looking for resolutions to problems or opportunities.

As is the case with the duality of human nature (self- and other-centered), I believe a well-functioning social network needs a mix of both bonding and bridging social capital. One is required to hold a group together and to provide a sense of common identity. The other is a necessary component to make a group reach out and become an essential part of more extensive networks. Balancing the two aspects is vital.

We can now see that the more social capital an organization or network is able to develop, the more things it can accomplish that others can only dream about. It's also apparent why there is such a critical relationship between social capital, self-organization, and the emergence and exchange of tacit knowledge. Most importantly, social capital is all about people fully realizing they are vital members of an internal and external network of mutually supporting individuals sharing tacit knowledge.

This by no means is intended to infer that challenges and disagreements are discouraged in these emergent and constantly evolving groups. In fact, the opposite is true. In an institution with a rich social capital base, new ideas and innovations are expected to be closely scrutinized by the network members, but in an atmosphere of trust and without attacking people personally. Challenges and disagreements are fundamental in assuring organizational and network vitality and success.

Fig. 3.3 Social capital dynamics

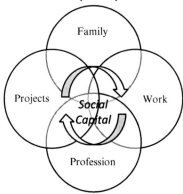

Social capital, also called coevolved relationships, is the most important element for any organization or network, particularly those that are knowledge based. As Fig. 3.3 depicts, social capital is an invisible yet extremely powerful organizational component that can't be duplicated by potential competitors. Every institution is composed of different individuals and a dissimilar collective "chemistry" that is self-sustaining and mutually reinforcing. Consequently, even if two businesses are roughly the same size and produce an identical product, they can never develop the same type and quality of social capital.

One of the most significant points to remember is that the more self-organization is practiced openly instead of being pushed underground, the more social capital an institution will generate.

The opposite is also true. The more structure and controls are imposed on an organization, by formal directives and direct supervision, the more the informal system will become covert and dispersed. Over time it may actually begin to undermine formal objectives rather than support them. The worst examples of this, of course, are the secretive social networks found in every prison. For instance, there is no prison in the world where the inmates don't have their own informal system of "laws" that are strictly enforced and which are completely hidden from the formal system.

Mergers provide a classic example of the vital importance of social capital and why overlooking this invisible asset can have serious consequences. In mergers, parties involved primarily deal with financial information or physical property in their analysis process – stuff that's tangible. They can't get their arms around the intangible assets such as the tacit knowledge that resides in the minds of organizational members. And forget about truly understanding and appreciating all the informal social networks that have evolved over the years.

Thus, what appears on the ledgers under "intellectual capital" (trademarks, patents, documented services or manufacturing processes, and so on) accounts for less than half of what these hidden assets are actually worth.

As a result, when a merger takes place and a new organization is assembled, the value of the intangibles that are the real foundation for the intellectual assets displayed on the books is usually not retained. Even if no employees are let go, most of the critical networks and their connections are usually at least partially severed, and no provisions are made to help establish new ones as quickly as possible. Even under the best of circumstances, it takes time for people to make new connections and the results are not guaranteed. Again, it's a self-organizing process that can't be managed.

Below are some of the key points to remember about social capital:

- It is the goodwill available to individuals and groups within social network.
- It provides valuable information, influence, and solidarity to the network members.
- It is a self-initiated drive by people to promote collective social interests.
- It increases in value with use.
- It can't be bought, sold, or traded.
- It is the wellspring of all new knowledge.

Identity and Personal Innovation Dynamics

Now that we have explored the attributes of the triad (evolved dispositions, tacit knowledge, and social capital), and the process of self-organization, it is now fitting to explore how the four fundamental features are linked.

To get a proper perspective of their interdependent dynamics, it is important to take into account that not only do these primary factors facilitate the development and maintenance of relationships and personal identities, but they also simultaneously impact the creation of ideas (ideation) at the individual level.

Figure 3.4 portrays the constantly evolving interdependent elements of the triad. What you can't see in this static picture is that the factors depicted in the model are always in a constant state of flux, and will continue to self-organize through circular causality.

Most critical is the fact that while the self-organizing process is taking place *between* the evolved predispositions, tacit knowledge, and social capital, circular

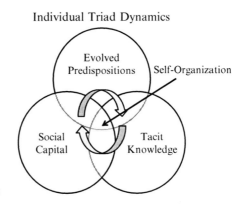

Fig. 3.4 Individual triad dynamics

causality is also constantly taking place *within* the factors themselves. That is, while the factors are evolving internally they are, at the same time, impacting each other. Again, we are not dealing here with customary linear cause-and-effect thinking – there is nothing linear about organic or living systems. All the elements come together and respond simultaneously.

So, let's take a closer look at the dynamics depicted by Fig. 3.4. For starters, our evolved predispositions are set in motion from the time of conception. Beginning in the womb, the primary repertoire of our neurological networks begins to develop through a process of cell division and purging. After birth these neural connections either strengthen or atrophy with use or lack of use as we engage the immediate world around us. Essentially, we end up with a cerebral cortex capable of conceptual categorization, memory, and learning in varying degrees, not to mention the myriads of lower functions over which we have very little or no control.

Our physical/mental makeup gives us the foundation for our individual personalities, which changes very little over a life time. Depending on the extent of our self - or other-centered experiences, we usually begin to express our evolved capabilities in three very general and overlapping ways.

First, we might become quite selfish if we grow up in a family where there is very little compassion to go around. That can be reinforced later by working in organizations where relationships are ignored and top-down goals and directives are strictly enforced.

Second, the reverse can also happen when a child who received an excess of empathy and caring grows up to unrealistically expect work relationships and other adult social interactions to be similarly indulgent.

Finally, there is a third way to express our innate drives: Both categories of our genetic predispositions can be expressed in a balanced fashion. In this instance, the environment is such that people are comfortable expressing a mix of both moderate self-interest and outward-reaching altruism. Most people prefer this type of balanced social context.

A word of caution is in order at this juncture. What I've just outlined are three very general categories of possibilities of our evolved capabilities or innate drives. Also remember that no two people are alike in the world. If follows then that no two people will respond in "exactly" the same way to identical biophysical and social environments, even if they are identical twins standing right next to each other in the same room. Something will be different.

Further, an individual may experience horrendous challenges early on yet still be capable of functioning in a very balanced fashion later in life. There is nothing linear about organic entities, although environmental contexts do have a significant impact on people's behavior as we will discover in the next chapter.

Tacit knowledge fits neatly into what we have looked at so far. From early on, as we go through life, we face all sorts of daily contingencies large and small. They all add up to experience. These experiences may involve sports, family events, work situations, love affairs, education, shopping, or being held up at gunpoint.

Our brains don't function like hard drives when it comes to memory storage. Instead, events that we experience are filed away in bits and pieces in various parts of our gray matter. Moreover, although all this information is embedded in related stories the accounts change over time as the events in the countless narrative become more and more entwined. That's why tacit knowledge comes in so handy, although it may also get us in trouble occasionally.

Essentially, our life experiences innately evolve into a macro model of the world around us. This grand perspective is a work in progress based on the "evolving" conceptual categorizations of our experiences stored in various locations of our brains. This tacit knowledge isn't easily accessed until we're faced with a new problem or opportunity where we can mix the "stew" to fit the situation. That's why tacit knowledge is also the wellspring of all new knowledge.

Conversely, if our tacit knowledge doesn't fit well with what we're faced, then we can easily go astray in selecting our available options. As we can all attest, not all experiences carry the same weight whether we're dealing personal finances or problems at work.

Let's summarize a few key points before we add social capital to the equation. It should be quite apparent that our evolved capabilities and accumulated tacit knowledge work hand in hand in a circular causality fashion. For instance, as parts of our genetic framework are strengthened or weakened through use so are our stores of tacit knowledge. Let me demonstrate this with a couple of brief examples.

Visualize for a moment that you're a pretty respectable amateur golfer. To maintain your level of competence (tacit knowledge) you golf at least three times a week. As a prominent scientist you're asked to participate in a project in Antarctica for a couple of months where you can't play golf. The nearest driving range is a thousand miles away. Undoubtedly, your golf game won't be the same when you return, at least for a while for the simple reason that your biophysical prowess for golf has diminished because of lack of practice. That is, your levels of tacit knowledge were reduced in the field of golf. Hence, the old saying, "Use it or lose it!"

Let's explore a similar question about work habits and work contexts. Imagine you have worked very successfully for the past 10 years for W. L. Gore & Associates, an organization which has no formal managers or supervisors. For whatever reason you decide to pull up stakes and join a tightly run hierarchical organization, like General Motors, where every person in the enterprise, with the exception of the CEO, reports to another person of higher rank. How much psychological tension would this new work environment create for you? Is it something you could overcome after working for Gore for 10 years? I'll attempt to answer these questions in Chap. 6. For now let's simply say that your world has most likely been turned upside down since your innate drives and tacit knowledge aren't attuned to the new environmental parameters.

Now let's add the third factor to the triad—social capital. Besides innately adjusting our genetic predispositions and tacit knowledge to our biophysical and social surroundings, we also begin to supplement our survival options with all sorts of informal support networks. In most cases, we are not even aware that we're gradually being drawn into these emergent webs. Our immersion into these support networks begins early in life first within the family. It then extends to family friends, church, school associates, friends at work, sports clubs, professional associations, and the list goes on.

The key thing is that these are all emergent, unplanned relationships. Reciprocity is the primary success factor in these informal networks. Also, with few exceptions an individual's membership in these loose alliances is seldom long lasting or permanent. As circumstances change, members continuously drop in and out of the maze of networks that confront them. The bottom line is that our hodgepodge of informal networks is crucial for our survival, no matter who we are or what we do. It's extremely difficult to survive as a hermit.

Finally, these emergent relationships give us the footing to establish and maintain our dynamic identities both for ourselves and for the people around us. Sit back and think for a moment what that means. For instant, you may walk around with a name tag, but that by itself doesn't give you an identity among the people you associate with. You earn your identity in varying situations. That is, you prove through your actions and behavior that you are an expert in some field, a good parent, an excellent teacher, a person that gives solid advice, and many other examples.

Identities are transient, not permanent. They are constantly challenged by the evolving biophysical and social environment around us. Accordingly, identities are based on perceptions, and their attributes are related to specific contexts.

A person earns and maintains multiple identities by trying to maintain some sort "personal comfort zone" around them. A person's personality is relatively stable, but identity varies depending on specific social contexts, e.g., being around a parent, a manager, or significant other. This variety of possible contexts requires continuous give and take with the people around you who, in turn, are also trying to maintain their own comfort zones.

Again, this is a serendipitous intrinsic activity usually not involving explicit negotiations. Here is another vivid example of why most of us prefer to live and work in productive social environments where people practice a mix of moderate self-interest and outward-reaching altruism.

The most salient points to remember from this chapter are:

- Relationships and identities are emergent and their outcomes can't be accurately predicted no less managed.
- Coevolving relationships and identities are founded on interpersonal exchanges and mutual trust.
- Identities are based on perceptions and their attributes are related to specific contexts.
- Systems designed to marshal group efforts and intelligence need to be flexible and guided by self-organizing principles.

In the next chapter, my primary focus will be on how to design a self-organizing system. Essentially, I'll demonstrate why the attributes of the triad are also the mainstay for innovation at the individual level, and what takes place when you combine the triads of a group of people in initiating a virtuous, as opposed to a vicious, cycle of innovation.

References

Adler, P. S. and Seok-Woo, K. (2002) "Social Capital: Prospects for a New Concept." *The Academy of Management Review*, Vol. 27, pp. 17–40.

Baily, K. (1987) *Human Paleopsychology: Applications to Aggression and Pathological Processes.* Hillsdale, NJ: Hove and London.

Berntson, G. G. and Cacioppo, J. T. (2008) The Neuroevolution of Motivation. In J. Shah and W. Gardner (Eds.), *Handbook of Motivation Science* (pp. 188–200). New York: Guilford.

Camazine, S., Deneubourg, J., Franks, N. R., Sneyd, J., Theraulaz, G. and Bonabeau, E. (2003) *Self-Organization in Biological Systems.* Princeton: Princeton University Press.

Dunbar, R. (1996) *Grooming, Gossip, and the Evolution of Language.* Cambridge: Harvard University Press.

Edelman, G. M. (1992) *Bright Air, Brilliant Fire.* New York: Harper Collins.

Ehin, C. (2005) *Hidden Assets: Harnessing the Power of Informal Networks.* Boston: Springer.

Goleman, D. and Boyatzis, R. (2008) "Social Intelligence and the Biology of Leadership." *Harvard Business Review*, September, pp. 74–81.

Hallowell, E. M. (1999) "The Human Moment at Work." *Harvard Business Review*, January-February, pp. 58-66.

Kluger, J. (2007) "What Makes Us Moral." *Time*, December 3, pp. 54–60.

LeDoux, J. (2002) *Synaptic Self: How Our Brains Become Who We Are.* New York: Penguin Books.

Linden, D. (2007) *The Accidental Mind.* Cambridge: Harvard University Press.

Nicholson, N. (2008) "Evolutionary Psychology, Organizational Culture, and the Family Firm." *Academy of Management Perspectives*, May, Vol. 22, Nr. 2, pp. 73–84.

Polanyi, M. (1958) *Personal Knowledge.* Chicago: University of Chicago Press.

Putnam, R., Feldstein, L. M. and Cohen, D. (2003) *Better Together: Restoring the American Community.* New York: Simon & Schuster.

Shubin, N. (2008) *Your Inner Fish.* New York: Pantheon Books.

Sternberg, R. and Horvath, J. Eds. (1999) *Tacit Knowledge in Professional Practices: Researcher and Practitioner Perspectives.* Mahwah, NJ: Lawrence Erlbaum.

Stevens, A. and Price, T. (1996) *Evolutionary Psychiatry: A New Beginning.* New York: Routledge.

Tudge, C. (2000) *The Impact of the Gene.* New York: Hill and Wang.

Wilson, E. O. (1998) *Consilience: The Unity of Knowledge.* New York: Knopf.

Chapter 4
Innovation Dynamics and Organizational Ecologies

In Chap. 3, we explored the major factors of the Triad (social capital, evolved predispositions, and tacit knowledge), and the interplay based on the principles of self-organization or circular causality.

In this chapter, we'll look at three related features to the overall framework, namely innovation at the individual, dyad, and organizational or network levels.

Individual Innovation Dynamics

Figure 3.4 depicted the dynamics of the Triad, shown again here as a reminder. Remember that the interplay of evolved predispositions, tacit knowledge, and social capital creates a constantly shifting sweet spot of self-organization where all three factors are present.

We can now advance that concept another step by showing how the Triad's dynamics directly shape a person's capacity to be innovative.

Figure 4.1 adds the component of "new environment" to the model and shifts the factors a bit. Just how does that change the equation?

Each person's Triad is not a steady, static system. Therefore, we are constantly evolving not only internally, but also externally as we come into contact with or become immersed in new biophysical and social settings. As individuals we must have enough flexibility, innovation, and variety in our social capital and tacit knowledge to accommodate changing environments and all the new and distinctive conditions they present.

As for evolved predispositions, being aware of our normal human inclinations helps us to accommodate change by providing a basic understanding of our needs and natural reactions to new conditions. An informed view of our human nature serves as a reference point and saves us from experiencing change as an unwelcome and chaotic intrusion rather than as an opportunity to grow.

In other words, each person's Triad must be sufficiently developed and flexible enough to deal with and adapt to new situations as they arise.

In speaking of the Triad from here on out, please understand that I am speaking of these as specific aspects within a whole person. I don't wish to imply that a

C. Ehin, *The Organizational Sweet Spot: Engaging the Innovative Dynamics of Your Social Networks*,
DOI 10.1007/978-0-387-98194-9_4, © Springer Science+Business Media, LLC 2009

Fig. 4.1 Individual virtuous cycle dynamics

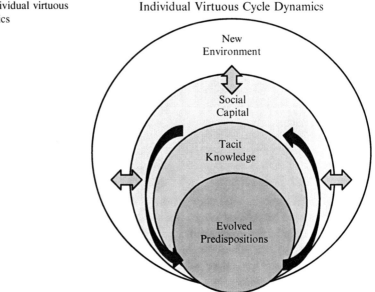

Individual Virtuous Cycle Dynamics

Triad is separate from the individual who encompasses it. It is merely the terminology I have developed to discuss the vital personal attributes that directly affect organizational dynamics.

Therefore, as individuals begin to adjust to the new contingencies, they first dig into personal stores of tacit knowledge to find a novel mix of ideas that will counter the fresh demands. In addition, when necessary they can access their established support networks, or social capital, for additional innovative approaches or to confirm the validity of their own proposed ideas and resolutions.

Accessing and using the Triad attributes helps an individual in several ways, but three appear to be most advantageous. First, the Triad serves as a protective shield when a person encounters a possibly dangerous situation. Second, it comes in handy when exploring new possibilities. Third, it's absolutely vital for developing and maintaining one's identity within constantly evolving social settings.

Dyad Innovation Dynamics

Now let's look at the innovation dynamics of a two-person relationship, or dyad. When two people interact to solve a common problem or take advantage of an opportunity, their Triads begin to overlap. Generally speaking, you are more likely to get more innovative and practical ideas from overlapping Triads than from separate individuals who are not interacting. Figure 4.2 provides a general depiction of two people in a virtuous cycle of innovation. The area of shared perspectives is where innovation is incubated and most productive.

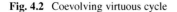

Fig. 4.2 Coevolving virtuous cycle

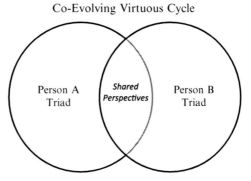

Co-Evolving Virtuous Cycle

Person A
Triad

*Shared
Perspectives*

Person B
Triad

What stands out in this instance is the perception gap. People's perspectives about a given situation are never exactly the same. Seldom are two people capable of experiencing a problem or situation in exactly the same way, which has both positive and negative implications.

On the negative side, the perception gap could potentially be so large that differences between the two participants would be irresolvable. Their established perspectives would be so far apart that they would not be able to close the gap. The distance would sink chances of innovation even before the individuals got started – the usual result of a vicious cycle.

The good news is that differing viewpoints are also the foundations for new and shared perspectives. If the overall relationship between the two individuals is fairly solid, then sharing the differing perspectives "creatively" becomes likely with the positive outcome of new perspectives and ideas all around. This is precisely what we expect to see as the result of a virtuous cycle.

So, how do new ideas evolve? They advance serendipitously by means of two simultaneous self-organizing processes. Initially, the Triads begin to overlap as people begin to share their ideas. Just as in the formation of the "shared-access domain" discussed in Chap. 2, the overlap is partial since it is impossible for two Triads to totally overlap.

As the conversations and information exchanges become more frequent and meaningful, each Triad expands. Because tacit knowledge and social capital increase with use, it's a win-win situation all around. An unforeseen problem gets solved, and both participants walk away with new perspectives, expanded tacit and explicit knowledge, and more widely extended social capital.

Organizational Innovation Dynamics

Now let's explore how the innovation process plays out at the organizational or extended network level. Figure 4.3 displays the key dynamics of a more extended virtuous cycle. The model is generic and can be used to analyze the general factors of any opportunity or problem solving event within a social group.

Fig. 4.3 Organizational virtuous cycle

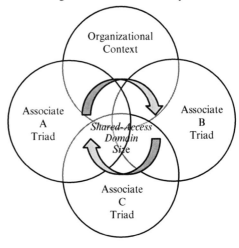

Much of what is depicted in Fig. 4.3 is very similar to the dyad virtuous cycle process. As members of an organization zero in on the problems, opportunities or goals of an organization or network, positive outcomes should emerge. That is, problems should get solved and organizational members should gain new perspectives, expanded tacit and explicit knowledge, and wider inclusion into a larger array of support networks.

These are, of course, the "ideal results" of an anticipated virtuous cycle. Unfortunately, the process can sometimes turn into a vicious cycle. What then turns a supposed virtuous cycle into a vicious cycle?

I suggest that most of the time it is because of fractured or nonexistent relationships and misperceived identities within an organization or an extended network of organizations. The major culprit for these splintered relationships usually is the managerial structure and the social environment that govern the enterprise's formal organization. (Note: other vocabulary you might see for managerial structure and social environment includes "organizational context," "organizational ecology," and "biophysical and social ecology.") Organizational context is the additional factor incorporated into Fig. 4.3.

Consequently, the various types of organizational contexts in which we live and work have a significant impact on the relationships and identities we develop and maintain. This poses an obvious dilemma.

Recall that in Chap. 1, I stated that it's possible to control organizational parameters, but not the behaviors of people within formal structures. That's the quandary. Organizational contexts matter but there is no precise way to determine how people will conduct themselves in dissimilar surroundings.

So, what do we do? Throw up our hands and surrender?

Not quite.

For the sake of a simplified illustration, let's assume you were fortunate to spend your early years surrounded by caring family members. Suppose they trusted you enough to allow you to experience a variety of social options from dating and joining clubs to participating in sports and school projects. Let's also assume you knew that no matter what happened your family would always be there to support you. In the process of growing up you gained personal confidence, enjoyed the benefits of close relationships, and learned to take responsibility for your commitments and actions.

Now imagine another person, perhaps a friend, who grew up in a family that was almost the opposite of yours. Assume there were daily disagreements and conflicts in your friend's family situation. When your friend needed help, he or she had no one to turn to because family members had little or no personal resources for empathetic care taking. The support system you enjoyed with your family was simply not there for your friend. Your friend did not gain confidence or enjoy the benefits of closeness, and consequently has difficulty in forming productive, mutually supportive relationships. Your friend is essentially adrift with weak social skills and a bleaker future than yours.

A word of caution: The two examples above portray "possible" outcomes, are for illustration only, and make sweeping assumptions. Examples of the opposite outcome abound. Many individuals grow up under the worst conditions yet develop into responsible and caring adults. Environmental contexts are important for successful outcomes, but it's also necessary to always allow for exceptions.

Organizational Macro Contexts

Let's now shift another step outward from family to organizational macro contexts. Here the same fundamental principles apply, but on a larger scale. Most people are familiar with all sorts of organizational structures and schemes advocated by countless management experts.

In my opinion, what these designs do best is create confusion.

As I taught graduate management courses and reflected on my past work experiences, defining organizational structures as tall or flat, vertical or horizontal, hierarchical or nonhierarchical, and so forth, became more and more frustrating. These descriptions seemed simplistic and relatively meaningless. They also appeared to imply that whether organizations were tall or flat, they were still predominantly top-down structures. The only differences were in the degree of hierarchy.

Eventually, I decided to describe organizational structures with two new terms: *controlled-access systems* and *shared-access systems*.

A controlled-access system, regardless of organizational tallness or flatness, is an organizational framework where access to all major resources is exclusively controlled by one person or a small group of people. All other members of the organization must first get approval from the appropriate authority, usually through a chain of command, before any of the assets can be used or invested. Leadership becomes a function of the position a person holds.

Most people in controlled-access systems are more concerned with their own welfare instead of the welfare of their coworkers or the organization. In such environments, people typically express more self-centered drives than other-centered drives. Competition between players is normal and is considered a necessary part of the game.

In controlled-access systems, *position power* is king, informal networks are not valued, and compliance rather than commitment is prized.

Conversely, in shared-access systems, all organizational members have considerable autonomy in decision-making and resource allocations, including hiring and firing personnel. Catalytic leadership (defined in the next chapter) emerges based on expert knowledge.

In shared-access systems, concern for self and others including the organization as a whole is well balanced. Expression of other-centered drives dominates and interdependence rather than competition is the preferred operational mode.

In a shared-access system, *expert power* rules, situational leadership (leadership defined by followership) and open book management are valued, and commitment rather than compliance is prized. Such an arrangement clearly benefits from expanded, mutually supportive relationships (social capital), and the continuous sharing of tacit and explicit knowledge.

Remember the "shared-access domain" or "sweet spot" introduced in Chap. 2? The shared-access domain has similar attributes as the shared-access organizational context. The shared-access context is specifically designed to "enhance" the expansion of the sweet spot within an enterprise. There, a flexible framework openly facilitates the self-organizing processes within the sweet spot and increases the rate of its expansion.

A shared-access domain is the area of an organization where the formal system's explicit requirements merge with the implicit needs and activities of the informal social networks through the process of self-organization. In this sweet spot, the formal and informal sides of an enterprise come together to enjoy "dynamic agreement" about the overall goals and processes of a venture. The two systems don't actually merge to become one. Instead, in the shared-access domain, circular causality becomes the predominant operating mode, with the formal and informal sides mutually affecting each other.

Most of the work in any enterprise gets done here. The sweet spot is inherently productive because it is relatively free from interference from the noncommitted elements of both the formal and informal sides of an organization. In the sweet spot, it's all about voluntary commitment, and not compliance.

Another vital but little acknowledged fact is that in any enterprise, organizational culture and identity evolves in the shared-access domain. Genuine cultures and identities can't be decreed or invented, although many companies spend a lot of time and money trying to do exactly that. Cultures and identities, like relationships, are emergent. They evolve over time and happen in the area where the productive action takes place - in the shared-access domain.

Two more defining points help identify organizations as either controlled - or shared-access enterprises. First, a controlled-access system is not a design that should be completely avoided or labeled as being "bad" or useless. It is definitely an option people can adopt as long as they are aware of its possible negative outcomes.

Second, each of these two macro categories represents an infinite number of possible organizational configurations. Each group and network is composed of different people, each functioning with different "chemistry." We'll explore this more deeply in Chap. 6 where I will describe four fundamental principles for developing flexible innovative organizations.

Now let's take a more detailed look at the attributes of both controlled-access and shared-access organizations.

Controlled-Access Ecologies/Contexts

Figure 4.4 depicts a typical controlled-access context. This is also what I call a "disengaged context," which will become more apparent shortly.

It should be evident that a controlled-access configuration isn't particularly participative, much less self-governing. As pointed out in Chap. 1, a hierarchical organizational chart like this one bears little resemblance to the actual relationships that form, and it can't come close to depicting how work really gets done. It actually depicts a mythical context with some very negative attributes, especially when it comes to member engagement and formation of relationships.

If you are in the position of building a shared- or controlled-access system, you must consider the level of engagement your organization needs or wants. If you want people to be as fully engaged mentally as possible, you will need to build an

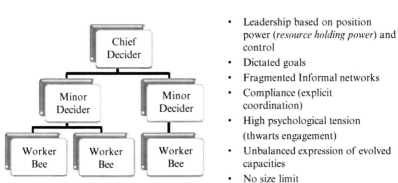

Fig. 4.4 Controlled-access ecology attributes (disengaged context)

organization that optimizes shared-access between the formal and informal aspects of the organization.

However, if mental engagement isn't a major necessity and people are hired primarily to just "move their hands and feet," building a controlled-access system is the most logical choice. Why? To answer that question, let's examine the list of each system's attributes to the right of the diagram.

First, in a controlled-access context, leadership is based on position power, or "resource holding power." What does this have to do with "real" leadership? Let me put it into a simple question. Does having the keys to a car give an individual the competence to drive the car? To refine the question further, does having the keys automatically give people the right to take the vehicle where ever they want to, select who can get into the car, designate where they can sit, and tell them when or where to get out? The quick answer might be, "If I own the car I can do anything I want to with it!"

But if you stop for a minute and think a little more deeply, you could ask if that's really practical and appropriate? What about the requirement to have a license, obeying the rules of the road and carry liability insurance? How courteous should the driver be toward passengers? How do the circumstances change if the car has been rented or if it happens to be a taxi?

Simply owning the resource isn't enough; evaluating how others are involved and affected is necessary and important. Even in a hierarchical controlled-access environment, it is important to consider productive engagement and the quality of relationships as part of the "perceived power" to tell people what goals and directives to follow. Unfortunately, such consideration is frequently not the case.

Hierarchies are necessary for managing rapid response organizations such as military units and large police departments, but they are not appropriate for all social endeavors. The problem with a hierarchy is that it is founded on two false assertions that ironically also serve as the foundation for its advocacy.

The first false assertion is that hierarchies are an unavoidable human phenomenon. This argument is true only if we prefer to rely primarily on the most primitive drives of the lowest level of our brain – the reptilian complex that evolved about 400 million years ago. If we believe that humans are more intelligent than reptiles, it would make more sense to rely on our characteristically social side, which is housed in more recently evolved, higher levels of the brain. This is especially true regarding our needs for social engagement, creativity, and innovation.

The second false assertion is grounded in the belief that social organizations can be developed and controlled to function like machines. The problem with this assertion is that it confuses control with order. Machines need external control mechanisms to maintain orderly functions. They are designed and constructed by humans, which can neither be 100% automated nor can they repair themselves to a significant degree.

On the contrary, people are not machines by any stretch of the imagination. They naturally self-organize around any situation or opportunity, establishing situation-specific order. They also have the capacity to "repair" themselves in most situations without external assistance.

Whether we want to admit it or not, hierarchical systems are artificial frameworks where actions and activities are points on a flow chart designed to depict mechanistic efficiency. In a controlled system, it is generally not thought necessary to consider and integrate our basic social/biological inclinations into planned organizational processes. In fact, it's humanly impossible to foresee and build into all the possible eventualities that members of a social system might encounter and may need to respond to. Thus, as we have seen previously, the charts are completely wrong when it comes to showing how work actually gets done.

Individuals respond according to what they perceive is happening in their immediate surroundings. No matter what the situation, people will self-organize according to their perceptions and what *they* believe is the most beneficial course of action, regardless of how an organizational chart or list of rules tells them to behave.

If, for instance, the circumstances seem to be nonthreatening and beneficial to the well-being of all involved, people will most likely share as much of their explicit and tacit knowledge as possible to solve a problem or take advantage of an opportunity encountered.

Conversely, if the state of affairs appears to have negative personal implications (such as someone else getting credit for a project), the people involved will put more effort into avoiding personal loss than on solving the overall problem.

Now let's take a quick look at some of the other attributes of a controlled-access context. I've already mentioned "dictated goals," where an authority spells out what the organization, group, or team goals are and how they must be carried out. Transactions are well prescribed, conversations are kept to a minimum, and relationships can be readily ignored.

Fragmented informal networks require a little more of an explanation. As I stipulated in Chap. 2, there are always two sides to every organization – formal and informal. In a controlled-access context the informal networks are present but usually not well connected to each other. For instance, the emergent groups in one location of a plant seldom connect with other groups in a different site unless they learn that they have extreme needs in common.

In a controlled-access scenario, management makes no effort to encourage these informal networks to interact freely for the benefit of the organization as a whole. In fact, some organizations try to suppress the activities of emergent entities because they can't be managed. In doing so, the entities go underground to form "clandestine operations," which can and sometimes do, undercut official goals and programs.

Compliance as opposed to commitment is another interesting feature of the controlled-access environment. Compliance dictates that every member of the venture should follow directions and directives to the letter, which is understandable and advisable when it comes to safety issues and guidelines. However, even with safety issues, instant deviations are appropriate during extreme life and death situations because of the unexpected circumstances.

When management tries to coordinate all normal day-to-day activities and interactions explicitly, people have very little incentive to initiate actions on their own. A strict compliance work context severely restricts innovation and curbs employees from voluntarily coordinating activities that may be beneficial.

Just imagine how much talent is wasted in such controlled systems. This is true especially when nonmanagement personnel are often aware of obvious problems they can help solve, or know of way to save vital resources and time, but are ignored because they are out of the management loop or because their solutions are not standard protocol.

High psychological tension is another trait of controlled-access contexts. High levels of psychological tension permeate such organizations because most members are anxiously competing for increased position power. Since position power is usually acquired through favorable individual assessments, the incentive to "look good" for high ranking executives is higher than the incentive to pursue collaborative activities, regardless of how mutually beneficial these activities may be.

In addition, people also nervously anticipate the next directive or policy to spring from the "head shed," wondering if it will enhance or weaken their position power in the organization.

The whole competitive atmosphere clearly thwarts not only cooperative social engagement, but also the ability of most people to more freely express and hone their talents.

Organizational size is the final attribute that needs consideration. Evidence clearly suggests that human beings are physiologically limited in developing and maintaining *voluntary* collaborative relationships in groups of more than 150 people. In larger collectives, relationships become fragmented and ties of common interest can't be properly sustained.

Face-to-face time is vital for mutual bonding and virtuous cycles. It's also essential for developing and expanding the shared-access domain enclaves that most likely exist within controlled-access systems.

Thus, from a human nature perspective, small organization size is vital for the development of supportive environmental contexts where informal groups and networks can flourish most effectively. Consequently, size can clearly be a problem for organizations wanting to boost efficiency and reduce cost by implementing mega-operations. Chapter 6 expands on organization size and its implications.

We have explored several aspects of the structure and attributes of controlled-assess systems and how they greatly increase the chances that people will disengage from their jobs. Hierarchies, position power, and resource control figure high in the disengagement equation as do dictated goals, fragmented informal networks, compliance, high psychological tension, and large group size. Appendix A provides more information about how to identify controlled-access systems.

Now it's finally time to begin revealing the secrets of shared-access systems and how they facilitate employee engagement.

Shared-Access Ecologies/Contexts

Controlled- and shared-access ecologies are not opposites of each other on a continuum. The two schemes are radically different and are on different, dissimilar scales. To understand it, you must make a quantum shift in thinking about organizational contexts.

In a controlled-access ecology, as Stacey, Griffin, and Shaw (2000, p. 105) help to clarify, "Managers seek to remove or suppress the conflicts that arise when people differ, seeing such conflict as disruptive to orderly process of change. It is all part of a framework of thinking, drawn from Newtonian logic and systems theories which equate equilibrium and harmony with success."

Conversely, shared-access ecologies attempt to function with living systems principles of self-organization based on our human need to independently and jointly express our identities and differences. As Stacey, Griffin, and Shaw (2000, p. 101) further explain, "The collective system conditions the response that any particular new behavior will receive, and this then leads to a characteristic restructuring of the collective system." It's all about circular causality. The shared-access system, just like the human body, functions without appointed managers.

Looking at Fig. 4.5, we can see that a shared-access system has roughly the opposite attributes as just outlined for a controlled-access context.

First, *leadership is founded on expertise and attraction* or social attention holding potential. It has nothing to do with position power or bossing other people around. Rather, in this context, leadership is situational in that everyone has an opportunity to take the lead depending on the situation. Leadership here is more about value-added facilitation rather than governing, which we'll explore in the next chapter.

Second, a shared-access system has *common goals* that are hammered out by all parties concerned and are constantly revised and updated as conditions change. Every member of the network or organization shares the responsibility for choosing and pursuing goals. It is a fully transparent and interdependent process.

Third, the *informal networks are codependent* and function in the open within and external to the shared-access framework. This suggests that all emergent social networks are *encouraged* to operate as visibly as possible instead of being pushed underground.

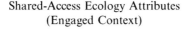

Shared-Access Ecology Attributes
(Engaged Context)

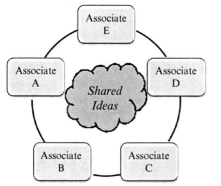

- Leadership based on expertise and attraction (*social attention holding potential*) & value-added knowledge facilitation
- Common goals
- Co-dependent informal networks
- Commitment (implicit coordination)
- Low psychological tension (promotes engagement)
- Balanced expression of evolved capacities
- Limited size (150 members)

Fig. 4.5 Shared-access ecology attributes (engaged context)

As a note of caution, when I say the networks are *encouraged* to function openly, I mean that literally. Emergent social systems adapt to change or stimuli much like amoebas changing shape when they surround food. Similarly, emergent systems will immediately respond to change or an outside disturbance by transforming and reshaping to fit the new situation. Because they adapt to changes so quickly, evolving informal networks *cannot be managed.* Because it's not possible to predict what the new structure will eventually look like, trying to manage informal groups makes little sense.

Thus, the members of a shared-access network have an incentive to freely connect with as many other networks as they see fit to support each other's activities, gaining more tacit knowledge in the process. Codependency in the informal networks is a powerful innovation generating dynamic and is important for expanding the shared-access domain.

Fourth, the shared-access system is *commitment-based*, which means that every member and team affiliated within this organizational context makes their own commitments and keeps them. A very simple yet powerful concept.

Think for a moment how diligently you attend to a task when ordered to do it vs. when you personally volunteer to do it. We already know that people are much more likely to complete a project they choose to undertake, and to do so enthusiastically. Of course, that also means that all the necessary coordination needed for a chosen project will most likely be accomplished implicitly and more judiciously. Employees are less likely to complete an assigned project successfully if they had no voice in making the assignment. It's a good example of the power of "unmanagement" in action.

Fifth, on the list of shared-access attributes is *low psychological tension*. Very simply, since this context is based on the principles of self-organization, its associated members are not all that concerned with the two big distractions that are part of the controlled-access system: "snuggling" closer and closer to the center of power (climbing the corporate ladder), and awaiting the next surprise announcement emanating from the inner sanctum of the CEO's office. Instead, the shared-access folks are mostly engaged with the tasks necessary to accomplish agreed-upon goals.

Sixth, *low psychological tension and a committed work environment* also make it much easier for all the network members to further expand and *express their own evolved capabilities in a balanced way*. The individual expanded capacities will in turn further increase the social capital of the organization and its capacity for innovation. The dynamics of the virtuous cycle cause it to constantly seek higher platforms and complexity to support overall network gains.

The Cherokee legend of Two Wolves from the previous chapter demonstrates the dynamics of our dual human nature. As one can see, in a shared-access environment, the "other-centered wolf" gets fed much more than the "self-centered wolf" to the benefit of everyone involved.

Finally, the shared-access system operates most effectively when its *size is limited* to roughly 150 core members. As stated earlier, face-to-face time is vital for mutual bonding and virtuous cycles. It allows people to select worthy and challenging problems to solve or opportunities to pursue.

In addition, as indicated in Chap. 3, face-to-face interactions involve more than just "simple" transactions and conversations. They also bring into play important physiological elements of our brains that are not activated in virtual exchanges.

Further, smaller size helps a group develop a constructive social ecology where members can practice a mix of moderate self-interests and outward-reaching unselfishness, which in turn leads to close personal ties and elevated levels of implicit coordination. This important factor helps maximize the shared-access domain throughout an organization, which is the intent for developing shared-access ecologies in the first place.

This doesn't mean that shared-access organizations are limited to 150 people. They're not. They can be of almost any size as long as their overall configuration is composed of small self-organizing units firmly connected to all the other entities of a venture. For best results, a uniform communications platform is needed that allows these small shared-access systems to be in touch with one another without the imposition of management schemes.

In summary, Fig. 4.6 graphically highlights the "shared-access domain" size differences between the controlled- and shared-access ecologies. It demonstrates why a shared-access system usually outperforms a controlled-access system in generating new and more practical ideas in responding to the demands of its biophysical and social environment.

Essentially, since close interdependent relationships are not openly supported within controlled-access ecologies, little tacit and explicit knowledge sharing takes place among its members. As a consequence, people have little chance of expanding or overlapping their personal Triads, resulting in a constricted volume of combined

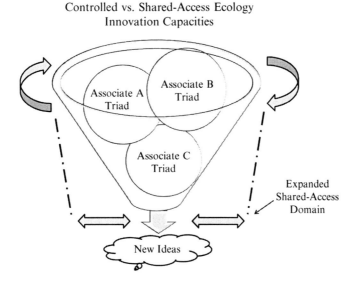

Fig. 4.6 Controlled vs. shared-access ecology innovation capacities

ideas trickling down from within a relatively narrow shared-access domain, as portrayed by Fig. 4.6.

Now imagine the social dynamics within a shared-access system. Extended interactions between informal network members within and external to the organization generate growing, catalytic interfaces among the participants. These exchanges expand every network member's triads. The individual triad expansions, in turn, also increase the size of the shared-access domain of the entire venture.

The result is that the total organizational innovation capacity constantly expands as depicted by the outward spreading of the funnel walls allowing more and more useful ideas to see daylight. This, again, is a good example why committed people regularly outperform those who are simply following management instructions.

The general success factors of shared-access ecologies are listed as follows:

- Shared goals and rewards.
- Autonomy to experiment with various options and to join multiple teams.
- Freedom to access and manage resources.
- Resolve to share ideas and value differences.
- Emphasis on expanding knowledge.
- Willingness to take responsible risk.
- Anticipating discontinuous change.
- Practicing catalytic leadership.

For more details about identifying characteristics of shared-access ecologies, please see Appendix B.

Looking ahead, how does one begin to develop a shared-access system where employees are truly engaged?

As you can surmise it is not an easy process and there are no guarantees. However, once such a system is up and running it exhumes the power of close relationships and an infinite capacity for innovation. I'll present four nonprescriptive general principles for the development of shared-access ecologies in Chap. 6.

The next chapter is entirely devoted to the subject of leadership. I will reveal the differences between what I consider to be true leadership vs. simple position power. In the process I will also define "catalytic leadership," which is the type of leadership critical to all shared-access systems and which facilitates rather than discourages engagement.

In the final analysis, keep in mind which "wolf" is predominantly fed either by the controlled-access or the shared-access organizational contexts as hinted by the Cherokee legend. I suggest that the Evil Wolf gets the nod for the controlled-access ecology and the Good Wolf matches well with the shared-access context.

References

Dunbar, R. (1996) *Grooming, Gossip, and the Evolution of Language*. Cambridge: Harvard University Press.

Ehin, C. (2000) *Unleashing Intellectual Capital*. Boston: Butterworth-Heinemann.

Sagan, C. (1977) *The Dragons of Eden*. New York: Random House.

Schoderbek, P. P., Schoderbek, C. G. and Kefalas, A. G. (1990) *Management Systems*. Boston, MA: Richard D. Irwin.

Stacey, R. D., Griffin, D. and Shaw, P. (2000) *Complexity and Management: Fad or Radical Challenge to Systems Thinking?* New York: Routledge.

Chapter 5
Leadership vs. Governorship

Genuine leadership has nothing to do with governorship, and the dissimilarities are significant. Most people, however, either don't distinguish or don't know the differences between true or intrinsic leadership and hierarchical position power.

In this chapter, I'll quickly review most of the "classical" and current leadership theories to give you a broad perspective of what is presently being taught in our business schools and concurrently applied in our business environments. I'll also define and suggest the type of leadership that seems to fit best with the dynamics of a shared-access system – one that is founded on commitment rather than on compliance.

Governorship is founded on position power and attempts to control people through *resource holding power.* In this scenario, appointed roles in organizations are controlled from the top-down, and the "higher ups" make all the status decisions about the people under them in the power chain.

That means someone higher up the power chain decides who gets promotions, the plumb office space, increases or decreases in salary, the best (or worst) assignments, and any other status-determining aspect of the work environment. Employees are often the unwitting darlings or victims of managerial whims and preferences. This type of governorship is an impediment to any self-organizing entity.

In contrast, *genuine leadership* is all about the pursuit of dynamic order, not control of others, and is based on coevolving interdependent relationships or self-organization. Emergent leaders earn their relative standings by means of *social attention holding potential.* In this scenario, leaders emerge naturally by using expertise, fresh perspectives, personal drive, responsible behavior, and any other "natural" attention holding attributes not related to any sort of coercive authority.

Real leadership is an emergent phenomenon that surfaces in all sorts of settings and unanticipated conditions. It's an unavoidable dynamic, just like the freewheeling formation of informal networks within any social endeavor. It is a vital dynamic of any social system, especially a well functioning or expanding shared-access domain within a shared-access organizational context.

Dave Snowden and Mary Boone (2007, p. 76) have rightly asserted that, "Business schools and organizations equip leaders to operate in ordered domains ... but most

C. Ehin, *The Organizational Sweet Spot: Engaging the Innovative Dynamics of Your Social Networks*,
DOI 10.1007/978-0-387-98194-9_5, © Springer Science+Business Media, LLC 2009

leaders usually must rely on their natural capabilities when operating in unordered contexts…In the face of greater complexity today, however, intuition, intellect, and charisma are no longer enough."

I suggest that people assuming leadership roles need a much more comprehensive grasp of human nature and its associated complex dynamics within different social environments. The power of emergent relationships needs to top the leadership agenda, not more refined control mechanisms.

Review of Management and Leadership Theories

We can find as many definitions of management and leadership as there have been writers on the subject. This fact suggests that leadership has no exact form that can be codified and precisely followed. As with personality, leadership style is a unique, tacit, distinctive part of every person that can't be fully duplicated in any other person. Consequently, countless "recognized" theories of leadership exist and more are added almost daily. So, let's briefly review management and leadership history, just to get our bearings before exploring new thought on the subject.

Starting with the Sumerians about 5,000 BC and continuing with the Egyptians, Chinese, Greeks, Romans, Venetians, and others, much has been written about managing large, complex organizations. Jumping ahead several millennia, during the Industrial Revolution, prominent economists and industry leaders such as Adam Smith and James Watt further advanced ideas about management.

Finally, at the beginning of the last century, three world-renowned figures set the stage for management thinking and research for the remainder of the Industrial Era: Max Weber, author of *The Theory of Social and Economic Organization*; Henri Fayol, who wrote *General and Industrial Management*; and Frederick M. Taylor, who became the leading management guru of his time with the publication of *The Principles of Scientific Management*.

In my opinion, management thinking since these classic works appeared almost 100 years ago has not truly progressed. Theories and methods developed since then have only refined the ideas presented by these three legendary authors.

Thinking about the topic of leadership has followed the same path as management. With rare exceptions, almost all of the research and literature on leadership have revolved around the "anointed" man or woman charged with the affairs of private or public institutions. That is, the focus since recorded history has been nearly exclusively on how best to attain and apply position power.

From a progression perspective, competition by intimidation and domination rather than by competition by attraction and voluntary cooperation has monopolized our accepted wisdom concerning leadership. Until very recently, rethinking simply hasn't even been in the cards. This is a good example of how research in any field seldom strays far from the conventional mindset. No wonder the "hidden assets" residing in every organization's informal social networks have been, and remain, largely untapped.

Classical Leadership Theories

Now let's take a closer look at some of the individual theories currently in use beginning with so-called "classical" theories of leadership. These theories are called classical because they have been around for quite some time, are part of the management curriculum of most universities, and are still widely employed in modern organizations. What they all have in common is that their center of attention is exclusively on assigned leadership or legitimized position power.

The coverage of classical leadership theories typically begins with the *trait approach*, originally designated as the "great man theory" before the introduction of equal opportunity laws. As you can probably speculate, considerable time and effort has been wasted on trying to define specific mental, psychological, and physical qualities associated with leadership success so that such a framework could be used to select "great men" for top positions.

Eventually, it was determined that leaders come in all sorts of shapes, sizes, and genders and that intelligence, self-confidence, courage, and so on also appear in a variety of forms. Obviously, the person in charge needed to have some aptitude but, other than that, the rest remained a mystery.

Today important traits are considered to be: decisiveness, knowledge, adaptability, integrity, sociability, and diplomacy. That, in my opinion, adds little to the usefulness of trait theories.

Next, we have the *behavioral theories* of leadership. These theories advocate that successful administrators shouldn't focus exclusively on either people or production; they must learn how to properly balance their attention on both. Still, it's clearly a top-down, position power orientation.

If traits and behaviors aren't enough to become a great captain of industry, we can turn to *Contingency Theory*. The contingency approach suggests that a good leader can determine what style of management to exercise by first determining what type of situation they confront. When that is decided, the managers then select one of three styles of leadership – task-oriented, relations-oriented, or a combination of both – to keep the troops in line.

Then, of course, there is the *Path-Goal Theory*. According to this theory, the leader's primary task is to define an employee's job and the best path to reach his or her work goals. The most appropriate way to do that is for the boss to match the right leadership style with the characteristics of the followers.

Finally, if all else fails, one can always turn to the *Life-Cycle Model of Situational Leadership*. A bright manager can apply this model by selecting one of four styles of leadership depending on the "readiness" of his or her followers. The styles include telling, selling, participating, and delegating.

And on and on with so many more classical leadership theories, models, and styles, I believe it is quite clear that, even under the most stringent top-down conditions, these guidelines can at best provide only limited benefit to aspiring administrators.

Modern Leadership Theories

Now let's explore some of the so-called "modern" theories of leadership that have surfaced in the past 15 years or so. One is *Super Leadership* which advocates encouraging followers to become self-leaders. There is nothing wrong with this concept except that the super leader doesn't give up his or her "throne" in the organization once everyone else has passed the self-leadership test. I suppose the super star has to keep his or her rank permanently, relatively speaking, to assure complete adherence to self-leadership.

The *Transformational Leadership* theory is still quite popular. This model suggests that excellent top executives must accomplish three things to keep their posts. First, they must recognize the need for organizational revitalization. Second, they must create a new vision. Finally, the transformation has to be institutionalized. Of course, this process is repeated again as conditions change. The question becomes how can Transformational Leadership be truly institutionalized without also seriously engaging the informal part of an organization where most of the work is accomplished in the first place?

The other four theories in vogue today are *Stewardship*, *Servant Leadership*, *Primal Leadership*, and *Level 5 Leadership*. Stewardship recommends that people in top positions guide followers into becoming responsible team players. Servant Leader proposes that leaders be willing to devote their efforts to serving others in accomplishing common goals. Primal Leadership suggests that positive emotions are contagious. Level 5 Leadership stipulates that the most effective leaders who help build enduring organizational greatness are not the high-profile types who make headlines, but are a contradictory mix of individual modesty and professional resolve.

How can anyone disagree with these leadership philosophies? Such leaders are absolutely vital in converting hierarchies into democratic or self-managing systems needed for today's knowledge economy.

However, what must also be plainly understood is that once the transformation is completed, these leaders, like everyone else, must relinquish their status based on rank (position power) and maintain their status in the group by adhering to the principles of emergent or "catalytic leadership," which I'll discuss shortly. Unfortunately, that isn't part of the deal outlined by these who advocate for the last four theories.

Four essential dynamics are key to the current theories of leadership. First, we need to admit that rank hierarchies are not the most efficient or human-friendly entities. The fact is that many social institutions can be changed to eliminate those deficiencies if we so desire. Second, whether flat or tall, run by a tyrant or a super leader, a hierarchy is a hierarchy no matter how its seats of power are masked.

Third, you can take the smartest and most charismatic person in the world and strap a supercomputer under each arm and they still could not be that ideal leader. Yet, strangely enough, we thoughtlessly expect the elected and appointed leaders in our public and private institution to accomplish that feat daily.

Certain leaders can be, and are in most instances, assisted by expert staffs in their decision-making processes. However, who makes the final decision, and how much does that individual heed the advice given to him or her? In many instances, aren't we literally setting people up for failure? Why don't we spread the organizational responsibility and accountability more evenly around instead of looking for a scapegoat when things go wrong?

If we are serious about developing much more effective enterprises, we need to be prepared to answer some pointed questions, and answer them honestly.

Finally, there is a very dark and seldom talked about side to the use of position power. Doling out rewards as bonuses, salaries, choice assignments, office space, etc. can be a very coercive exercise, even by well-meaning people.

Much more demoralizing is the frequent application of position power or sanctioned (legitimate) hierarchical power. There really is no such thing as position or legitimate power. The only way a person is able to have more authority over others is for people working with them to either willingly, or by some form of intimidation, give up some of their individual influence. In other words, for someone to gain power over his or her social group its members need to first relinquish a significant portion of their own decision-making capacity.

In any case, the more frequently people use position power, the more comfortable they usually become wielding authority over others. Eventually these individuals begin to devalue their subordinates by attributing their performance to their own prowess rather than the abilities and motivation of their underlings. Repeated users of position authority also like to maintain psychological distance from their employees and begin to believe that it's acceptable to use manipulative schemes for leadership effectiveness.

Position Power vs. Catalytic Leadership

Position power is founded on coercion, no matter how benevolent, and demands compliance from subordinates in following directives. Genuine leadership is situational and based on talent, expertise, and the demands of a particular circumstance. Hence, it is reliant on the commitment, not compliance, of followers in fulfilling mutually agreed-upon goals. Also, the followers involved in a specific engagement or project don't relinquish their autonomy. They are free to disengage at any time. As one can see, the differences are significant.

Genuine leaders are able to perceive certain situations from a different or clearer and less ambiguous perspective. They have a strong drive and willingly assume personal responsibility to complete a task, solve a pressing problem, or to seize an opportunity. Accordingly, such leaders can take a confusing or complex state of affairs and frame it in a particular way that enables others both to understand it and willingly take appropriate action. Trust is also an important aspect of true leadership. Versatile leaders are well aware of the value of this quality, and trust people based on their expertise, proven record of accomplishments, and codependent relationships.

True leadership also has an underlying genetic or neurological component. As pointed out in Chap. 3 parts of our neural networks include mirror, spindle, and oscillator cells that respond in a certain fashion in both the leader's and followers' brains. As Goleman and Boyatzis (2008, p. 76) stipulate:

> …certain things leaders do-specifically, exhibit empathy and become attuned to others moods-literally affect their own brain chemistry and that of their followers. Indeed, researchers have found that the leader-follower dynamics is not a case of two (or more) independent brains reacting consciously or unconsciously to each other. Rather, the individual minds become, in a sense, fused into a single system.

Thus, leadership is less about social "skills" than it is about having an innate talent for nurturing positive feelings in people whose help a person needs. Leadership, therefore, has significant physiological factors that come into play, as is true for relationships in general.

Goleman and Boyatzis further suggest that "the only way to develop your social circuitry effectively is to undertake the hard work of changing your behavior." Here they are essentially referring to our genetic predispositions and their individual "set-points" briefly discussed in Chap. 3. What they suggest people should do if they have low personal set-points in empathy and attunement is to consciously work on increasing them through coaching and daily interactions with others.

I fully support this approach if it includes everyone in an organization. However, what Goleman and Boyatzis seem to advocate is limiting this training/coaching to people in leadership positions. That's not only strange, but is borderline unethical. My reasoning is simple. If the "neural chemistry" or physiology applies equally to all members of an enterprise, then why should only a privileged few be included in the training?

To me that just smells bad. It appears to be training a small group of people to be better manipulators. That's not only unethical in my book, but also detrimental to the effectiveness of the entire organization. Constructive relationships are beneficial to everyone not just "assigned" leaders.

It is my contention that anyone of sound mind and body is capable of being a leader. Depending on their talents, skills, and experiences, certain people are able to assume leadership roles more often than others, but each one of us has the capability to lead. The opportunity may be a small event or something monumental. When and what a person takes charge of depends on their background, chance, the group involved, and the situation. Thus, whether a person is a world-renowned expert or a novice they can and should take the leadership wheel when the right occasion presents itself.

Emergent leadership is a requisite and inevitable component of human social groups. It is a natural dynamic part of the self-organizing process of all biological entities.

Position power, however, is not. It is an imposition and is dealt with accordingly (politely or otherwise) by the people associated with it. Consequently, from my standpoint, designated leaders can rarely be considered "genuine" leaders. Only emergent leaders have earned the respect of the people who willingly follow them. That esteem also constantly needs to be reacquired as conditions change because, unlike position power, emergent leadership is situational and fluid.

Essentially, "no bossing" leadership is a vital dynamic of a shared-access social system, especially within the shared-access domain of such an organizational ecology. From my perspective, however, none of the leadership theories reviewed previously is fully capable of supporting the coevolving relationships fundamental to all self-organizing entities. Why? The simple answer is that they are not based on emergence founded on circular causality.

As a result, I'm advocating for what I call "catalytic leadership." As the name suggests, catalytic leaders "enable," but don't *force or demand* change. Instead they *enable* needed processes or necessary changes to take place. As a result, change happens much more quickly and effectively than otherwise possible under traditional leaders. Thus, they are agents that provoke or speed up productive "emergent activities" within a free flowing social system.

Such leadership is characterized by "catalytic" behavior (involving or causing an increase in the rate of action and interaction by group members without the imposition of one's will) of individuals attempting to facilitate the integration of people's personal goals and aspirations with the aspirations a venture as a whole. It's a process of continuous change where different individuals (depending on their talents, skills, and expertise) are looked to for guidance and advice when a group is faced with different internal and external circumstances. It is founded on voluntary actions intended for mutual benefits and involves no intimidation or bossing. *In essence, no one gives up his or her autonomy or power in the process.* I define catalytic leadership as:

> Encouraging others to participate in value-added activities they are either not aware of or are hesitant to initiate on their own, that would benefit everyone involved.

It may appear that I dislike hierarchical systems. I don't. People determine how best to organize their collective endeavors. I simply want to highlight what I consider to be a more effective option for running our social institutions besides the top-down hierarchy.

Our decisions on how to make that choice should rest on solid evidence and not on myths or misinformation.

We also should keep in mind that workers in general and knowledge workers in particular are most productive when they labor in an environment where they can practice a mix of moderate self-interests and outward-reaching unselfishness leading to close personal ties and elevated levels of implicit coordination. Catalytic leadership is a vital component of such social contexts.

Catalytic Leadership Dynamics

Now let's take a closer look at the major dynamics of catalytic leadership. Figure 5.1 highlights the four key interactive elements of the leadership dynamics.

You will notice that as with the other models, four general attributes interact and overlap to create dynamic relationships to solve common goals. In this model, the four attributes are emergent leadership capacities, peer support, opportunities and problems, and shared-access context. We'll explore each attribute and how they effectively interact.

"Emergent leadership capacities" encompass the first element of the model. As is the case with our personalities, leadership qualities are partly genetic and partly gained through life experiences. Hence, we all have leadership potential to one degree or another.

For example, some of us may be more extroverted, conscientious, or open-minded than our colleagues. The same applies to our talents. One person may be naturally inclined toward instant action or going for the gold instead of being satisfied with average results. Another may be more interested in continuous learning and seeking meaningful connections with the world around them. At the same time, a third individual may be engaged in advancing the frontiers of science.

All of us need to discover our natural predispositions and put them to productive use. Regrettably, countless people are more concerned with overcoming their deficiencies rather than leveraging their inherited abilities. Therefore, it's wise to keep in mind that leadership development follows personal growth. As each individual experiences personal growth, leadership ability increases incrementally. It is a progression whereby individuals with different traits and experiences will emerge to orchestrate activities as each diverse situation demands.

As we all instinctively know, no one person has the capacity to be an effective leader under all circumstances. Since circumstances and individuals are infinitely different, the incalculable variety of possibilities dispenses with that possibility.

From a human nature perspective, individuals with the "right stuff" – specific talent, skills, and know-how – attract other people depending on varying circumstances. That is, people are always on the lookout for other folks who may complement or enhance their particular talents and skills with their divergent capabilities.

Therefore, everyone needs to be prepared to take the lead when a fitting situation presents itself. In fact, members of a self-managing group will look for and expect to receive advice and guidance from individuals who have expertise or experience in a particular area depending on the state of affairs. It's an implicit reaction and has nothing to do with personal submission.

This leads us to the peer support component. In general, we are naturally inclined to attempt to some degree to "mind-read" and keep track of the behavior of others.

Thus, group members have a predictable penchant to evaluate who has the right stuff and under what conditions. Specifically, this means that the associates (as opposed to employees or followers) are constantly observing and categorizing the actions and reactions of their colleagues in dissimilar circumstances. Again, it's all about circular causality instead of cause-and-effect thinking.

These tacit peer assessments, however, are made in an atmosphere of trust and mutual support rather than vying for "upsmanship." In a shared-access system, there is no incentive to climb the ladder because there is no ladder to climb. Rather it's all about helping others to achieve reciprocally beneficial goals with the clear understanding that everyone in the group needs to be prepared to take the lead depending on the situation. Hence, people look for unique qualities in each member that can be leveraged for the benefit of the entire group.

You can begin to see why diverse sets of individuals in a self-organizing organization outperform those that are more homogeneous and why everyone has the capability, at least occasionally, to assume a leadership role. Further, individual identities and status stem from activities that attract others and are neither absolute nor permanent. As conditions and needs change, so can an individual's identity as a prospective catalytic leader.

In a self-organizing environment, people needn't relinquish or surrender their autonomy even temporarily under any circumstances. At the same time, however, every member also accepts full responsibility and accountability for the success or failure of the entire group.

Thus, in a shared-access system everyone should be well aware of their associates' abilities. This assures that each member of a group knows when to take the lead and when to follow. It is also important that associates continuously pursue personal development individually and in teams. After all, self-organization is about positive coevolving relationships not compliance.

Next we need to briefly focus on the "opportunities and problems" component of the model. Fundamentally, this suggests that the need for leadership exists only when there is an identified organizational opportunity to track or a specific problem to solve. In a self-managing system, every member is constantly trying to discover new possibilities and to detect potential problems that may need attention.

These situations may first be investigated independently or immediately brought to the attention of other associates. It all depends on the potential dimensions and effect the situation may have on the venture.

Essentially, each group member is responsible for exploring any positive or negative state of affairs that he or she happens to encounter. If the member uncovers a possibly worthwhile new undertaking, he or she initially can independently scrutinize it or immediately solicit support from other interested people.

In any case, once enough people become convinced that a project is worth pursuing, the associate who made the original discovery usually will assume the lead role in the project if he or she feels that they have the right qualifications. Thus, emergent order develops around the project from start to finish.

Shared-access context is the fourth element depicted in Fig. 5.1. Emergent leadership is seldom officially recognized and sanctioned within top-down systems.

Fig. 5.1 Catalytic leadership dynamics

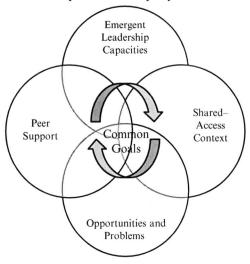

It is always present but, like a black market, it functions in the shadows or underground. As a clandestine operation, there are no assurances whether the informal leadership supports, undermines, or simply stays neutral when it comes to formally declared policies and goals.

Simply put, the realizations of the full benefits of social engagement are slim to impossible to attain without a shared-access organizational context that openly promotes and supports catalytic leadership. Such an environment is dependent on the development and maintenance of four vital tenets (discussed in detail in the next chapter). They include giving associates a great deal of autonomy to broaden their own unique identities, developing and maintaining a shared organizational identity, assuring members embrace challenging mutually supportive goals, and practicing dynamic alignment. The major emphasis is on catalytic leadership and interdependent thinking. As one can see, there is no place for governorship in a shared-access system.

Finally, "common goals" are at the central core of the model that integrates the entire catalytic leadership process. It is the nucleus around which the four key elements concurrently revolve in a complementary and dynamic manner. Without mutually agreed-upon overall organizational intentions, the framework falls apart. Without common goals, opportunities and problems that surface have no reciprocal appeal. It is similar to a "country club" environment. Everyone is out to have a good time, but only for his or her own amusement. There is no need for unrestrained trust and reciprocity.

In the next chapter, I'll suggest how to develop a shared-access work environment based on the four tenets mentioned above. My recommendations will be descriptive rather than prescriptive because no organization or network is ever precisely identical.

References

Bedeian, A. G. (2002) "The Dean's Disease: How the Dark Side of Power Manifests Itself in the Office of Dean." *Academy of Management Learning & Education*, December, Vol. 1, Nr. 2, pp. 164–173.

Block, P. (1993) *Stewardship: Choosing Service over Self-Interest*. San Francisco: Berrett-Koehler.

Block, P. (2008) *Community: The Structure of Belonging*. San Francisco: Berrett-Koehler.

Boon, L. E. and Bowen, D. D. (1987) *The Great Writings in Management and Organizational Behavior*. New York: Random House.

Collins, J. (2002) *Good to Great*. New York: Harper Business.

Ehin, C. (2005) *Hidden Assets: Harnessing the Power of Informal Networks*. New York: Springer.

English, F. W. (2008) *The Art of Educational Leadership*. Thousand Oaks, CA: Sage.

George, C. S. (1972) *The History of Management Thought*. Englewood Cliffs, NJ: Prentice-Hall.

Goleman, D. and Boyatzis, R. (2008) "Social Intelligence and the Biology of Leadership." *Harvard Business Review*, September, pp. 74–81.

Goleman, D., Boyatzis, R. and McKee (2001) "Primal Leadership: The Hidden Driver of Great Performance." *Harvard Business Review*, December, pp. 42–51.

Pierce, J. L. and Newstrom, J. W. (2000) *Leaders and the Leadership Process*. New York: McGraw-Hill.

Senge, P. (1990) "The Leader's New Work: Building Learning Organizations." *Sloan Management Review*, Fall, pp. 7–23.

Snowden, D. J. and Boone, M. E. (2007) "A Leader's Framework for Decision Making." *Harvard Business Review*, November, pp. 68–76.

Stevens, A. and Price, T. (1996) *Evolutionary Psychiatry: A New Beginning*. New York: Routledge.

Chapter 6
Unmanaging Relationships and Innovation

Information and expertise become outdated faster than fashion trends these days in our current knowledge-intensive environment. Consequently, today people are valued more and more for their abilities not only to learn, but also to quickly unlearn and relearn. A shared-access context helps individuals and teams to do that far better than any configuration of a controlled-access system.

I'm convinced that shared-access systems are the most productive organizational environments for riding the waves of rapid and erratic change so common in our twenty-first century.

At the end of Chap. 4 we explored the differences between two diametrically opposed macro organizational ecologies – the controlled-access and shared-access systems. In this chapter, we'll explore a general framework for developing and maintaining shared-access contexts as a means to more fully engage the people who work in them.

Expanding the Shared-Access Domain

Shared-access organizational contexts are founded on nondeterministic principles.

Shared-access context is the direct opposite of firm management structures designed to control the behavior and interactions of its members. Shared-access supports relationships between people in their various roles as much as possible rather than attempting to manage, control, or limit those relationships.

It supports and enhances the self-organizing "authentic behavior" of its participants rather than the mandates of a flow chart. Shared-access focuses on the day-to-day reality of people's actual roles, transactions, conversations, and relationships rather than on the "fantasy" of how things are supposed to work according to some grand management plan.

A shared-access organizational environment is specifically designed and continually adjusted to facilitate the expansion of the shared-access domain within a venture as depicted by Fig. 6.1. Since it is self-organizing, the shared-access domain can't be managed, but it can be influenced by its environmental contexts.

C. Ehin, *The Organizational Sweet Spot: Engaging the Innovative Dynamics of Your Social Networks*,
DOI 10.1007/978-0-387-98194-9_6, © Springer Science+Business Media, LLC 2009

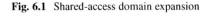

Fig. 6.1 Shared-access domain expansion

Shared-Access Domain Expansion

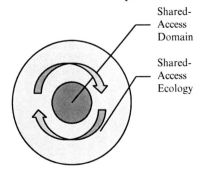

Just like individuals, self-organizing social systems respond to intimidating environments quite differently than they do to supportive environments.

Remember, too, that it's not possible to completely overlap the formal and informal systems. All ventures need some uniformly recognized policies and procedures so that effective transactions and conversations can take place. This formal framework keeps the organization running smoothly and can't be fully eliminated. A venture cannot be wholly immersed in the shared-access domain.

Also, depending on the overall biophysical and social context of an organization, not all of the informal networks will participate fully in the shared-access domain activities. A certain number of people will always be disengaged from productive work, busy doing such things as developing mutually supporting relationships or gaining a footing for their identities. This means that no matter what allowances are made, not everyone on the informal side of an organization will be fully engaged in the sweet spot activities.

Whether situated in a controlled- or shared-access system, a shared-access domain will make its own adjustments no matter what is "formally" demanded. Therefore, it's important to give considerable attention to using nondeterministic principles in developing and adjusting shared-access contexts. To ignore such principles usually results in little or no movement away from a controlled-access organizational structure.

Principles Supporting Shared-Access Systems

Expansion of shared-access domains within an organization or network relies on four *overt* self-organizing principles. The principles are theoretical constructs created with the aid of four primary sources:

- Anthropological studies of immediate-consumption hunter-gatherer social systems
- Identification of critical elements required for small groups to be able to self-organize
- Chaos theory
- Complexity theory

These principles are the very foundation for the development and maintenance of shared-access systems.

Anthropology

From my years of study and analysis of anthropological data, I have identified five fundamental organizational success factors our hunter-gatherer ancestors relied on for roughly 200,000 years. They are "immediate-consumption" factors because high mobility and limited storage capabilities dictated that they consume what they gathered within 48 hours. Our ancestors were successful largely because:

- They lived in relatively small, very interdependent groups composed of kin and close friends.
- They maintained high sustained levels of reciprocity, egalitarianism, and practiced consensus decision-making.
- Members owned their own means of production.
- They respected individual autonomy and self-reliance tempered with high levels of social responsibility and accountability.
- They practiced situational, or what I have labeled catalytic leadership, based on expertise (social attention holding power) rather than rank or position power (resource holding power). They also did not base status differences on gender.

What stands out about these five factors is that for hundreds of thousands of years, primitive humans maintained fluid social structures based on self-organizing principles. Based on that fact, we can assume that these people developed greatly expanded triads specifically geared toward their environment, and that their personal triads also overlapped considerably due to their close relationships to one another. This seems to be the primary reason why most people even today are most comfortable working and living in social contexts where there is a balance between moderate self-interests and outward reaching altruism.

Even more revealing about our ancient past are the recent cross-cultural studies conducted by Bradley University psychology professor Davis Schmitt and his international colleagues. They are discovering that since our hunter-gatherer ancestors were relatively egalitarian, "Humanity's jaunt into monotheism, agriculturally based economies, and the monopolization of power and resources by a few men was 'unnatural' in many ways."

Their research indicates that people are beginning to act more innately in societies where the psychological stressors of traditional highly paternalistic top-down rule-oriented ways of life are reduced. They cited the USA and the Netherlands as examples of such societies. "In some ways modern progressive cultures are returning us psychologically to our hunter-gatherer roots." Said another way, once the unnatural barriers are removed, people begin to engage each other in more fundamentally intrinsic ways.

I suggest that we need to develop organizations that function more "naturally" far more rigorously than we do now.

Self-Organization in Small Groups

Smith and Comer determined that four key elements are necessary for self-organization to take place in small groups. First, sufficient interaction (or periphery openness) between group members and the immediate environment must be present. Second, participants need to have an investigational aptitude or willingness to learn. Third, the group must be attentive to a deep common vision and values (or individual and group self-reference). Lastly, group members must have a shared identity, meaning they have a capacity to move as a whole adjusting to changing conditions as necessary. These elements run neatly parallel to the hunter-gatherer success factors.

Chaos and Complexity

Two other factors enter into the mix of shared-access success: chaos and complexity. Chaos and complexity theories, in extremely simplified form, make some very fitting generalizations about groups as adaptive coevolving systems. We see how emergent groups fit squarely into these theories.

A system can be as small as a single cell or as expansive as the universe and beyond. However, for our purposes here, we'll consider individuals or groups of individuals as systems.

Chaos theory tells us:

- A system (a person or group) is unpredictable and bounded at the same time. The system never goes beyond certain margins; it has a self-reference to which it always returns.
- Systems never attain true equilibrium, since they are very sensitive to small disturbances all the time, and are never precisely the same twice.
- Complexity theory tells us:
- Nonlinear and unpredictable systems such as people and groups are more complex than linear, cyclical, and predictable machine-like structures.
- Growth can't happen unless systems are in a state of disequilibrium.

In other words, a system cannot change and improve if it's predictable and balanced. A slightly chaotic system is always out of balance and unpredictable, and always shifting to meet the challenges of change. As disorder increases within a system, the disequilibrium reaches a point where the system abruptly shifts, breaks down, and restructures itself into a more viable configuration than it was before. Both creativity and destruction are an integral part of this emergent process.

We've seen chaos and complexity before in shared-access groups. An individual's behavior is never exactly the same but, at the same time, his or her behavior is bounded by unique identity attributes of skills, personality, and physical traits.

Fig. 6.2 Shared-access ecology tenets

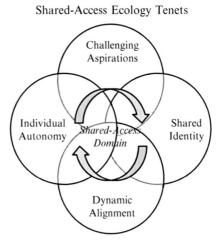

Shared-Access Ecology Tenets

Challenging Aspirations

Individual Autonomy

Shared-Access Domain

Shared Identity

Dynamic Alignment

In a self-organizing group, individual autonomy is constantly tempered by social responsibility and accountability.

So you begin to see why efforts to use linear and deterministic mechanisms to control nonlinear frameworks make little sense. The message for today's organizations (and this was also applicable to the hunter-gatherers) is that since they must interact with a constantly changing, information-rich and complex environment, they must be equally multifaceted and flexible in order to survive. It's quite apparent why structures founded on a cause-and-effect or machine metaphor have an adverse affect on complex organic beings, such as humans.

Chaos and complexity theories have been incorporated into an integrated practical framework shown in Fig. 6.2. Any organization can use the model to increase the levels of interdependent relationships and the willingness to share tacit and explicit knowledge.

However, the dynamic arrangement is *descriptive, not prescriptive*, since every organization is unique and functions in a different biophysical and social environmental. Each social group needs to determine how to develop and apply the four self-organizing principles in their own distinctive way.

The most important aspect regarding the model is that it is extremely vibrant and interdependent. It is a parallel operating system in which the four tenets of individual autonomy, shared identity, challenging aspirations, and dynamic alignment function together simultaneously. The overlap again forms the optimum shared-access domain or sweet spot.

Thus, such an "overt" self-organizing system works best when the attributes of each tenet have been developed to a considerable extent and placed in motion within its network of members. The dynamics of the process are all about expanding the shared-access domain as much as possible.

A closer look at these four tenets will help build an understanding of how they work together as a complex adaptive system.

Individual Autonomy

To gain positive self-organization (as opposed to the underground type which can be positive, neutral, or negative), an organization or network needs to be composed of self-reliant people who are able and willing to take responsibility for their actions. These people also need to function both independently and in multiple teams, depending on the circumstances as their roles and identities become clearly established.

The system is comprised of partners or associates whose activities and interactions are founded on personal relationships and commitments and not on compliance with top-down directives. A partnership also requires that each affiliate contribute something valuable to a venture. In effect, the system is extremely dependent on two interrelated qualities – interdependence and reciprocity.

The bottom line is that it's not particularly easy to work in a shared-access system. Individuals who have become accustomed to functioning in "9 to 5" or controlled-access mode have great difficulty in accepting the high levels of personal responsibility and accountability in a self-organizing framework. There is no place for "hired hands" in a shared-access system because there are no bosses to issue directives or "employees" to carry them out.

All this requires a high degree of selectivity in determining who should be asked to join an organization. Being very selective has nothing to do with being arrogant or "snobbish." Every organization needs to screen people one way or another to at least assure it hires people who have the talent and skills to fill an institutional need.

Key considerations in personnel selection:

- *Talent and expertise.* Individuals joining the organization need a diverse set of talents and skills, including social skills to support and compliment the needs of other members.
- *Role responsibility.* Each member needs to be willing to take responsibility and accountability not only for their own roles, but also for the actions of the entire organization.
- *Personal autonomy and commitments.* Individual autonomy and identity are highly valued. However, associates need to be capable of working both on their own and in teams. Above all, they need to be willing to make their own commitments and keep them.
- *Social responsibility.* Members are expected to be self-reliant and pursue sensible self-interests. Conversely, they also need to practice far-sighted self-sacrifice in helping others and the organization succeed.
- *Empathy and attunement.* Associates need to be empathetic and attuned to what motivates other people, even if they don't agree with them. They also need to pay attention to what others around them think and feel.

Shared Identity

Every close-knit social entity develops a unique shared identity or special chemistry that binds it together through good times and bad. An established organization or network is a distinctive living and breathing biological system with its own needs and goals trying to survive as best it can in its particular environment.

This shared identity is unique for two reasons. First, as far as we know, no two people born on our planet have ever been entirely identical. So it follows that no two groups could ever be alike. Groups are guaranteed to have distinctive members and identities.

Second, after a group is formed, it begins to develop unique voluntary connections between its members as they self-organize.

Clearly, the more open this coevolving process remains, the more constructive and organization-specific these networks become throughout an enterprise. According to Watts (2003, p. 115), "All the things we do, all the features that define us, and all the activities we pursue that lead us to meet and interact with each other are contexts. So the set of contexts in which each of us participates is an extremely important determinant of the network structure that we subsequently create."

Also recall from Chap. 3 that people seem to function best in a constructive social context where both the self- and other-centered innate drives can be freely expressed in a balanced manner. It's an environment where individuals freely engage one another with a mix of both moderate self-interest and outward-reaching altruism. This type of social context promotes implicit coordination and is also vital for sharing tacit knowledge.

Further, ample research by Professor Robin Dunbar and others indicate that groups of about 150 or fewer are best for creating positive relationships. We humans are physiologically limited in our ability to develop and maintain voluntary collaborative relationships in larger groups. In those scenarios, relationships become fragmented, ties of common interest can't be properly sustained, and hierarchical structures tend to creep in. Thus, from a human nature perspective, small group size is vital for the development of constructive interactive environmental contexts where informal groups and networks can flourish most effectively.

Therefore, overt (as opposed to covert) self-organizing systems can normally only be realistically nurtured within relatively small groups. A strong sense of interdependence can only be developed in an environment small enough where everyone can maintain face-to-face or line-of-sight relationships with all group members. The best sign that people are maintaining excellent face-to-face interactions is when everybody calls each other by their first names.

Small group size is especially critical for innovation and the transfer of newly acquired knowledge to other people. There is no better way to diffuse innovative ideas and processes than direct face-to-face communications in an environment laden with interpersonal trust. This has been further confirmed by the recent study of professors Vibha Gaba and Alan Meyer (2008, pp. 994–995). They state:

Given the entire furor over innovation and upheaval, it is worth noting that our study's central finding is a time honored truism. Even in a world of digital information, outsourced work, distributed decisions, and global supply chains, it is reassuring to discover that innovative approaches to innovating still spread best when people in richly connected social networks come into direct physical contact, get acquainted, and exchange analog data.

This, however, doesn't mean that meaningful collaborative relationships can't be fostered within large organizations and extended virtual networks. Enterprises comprised of more than 150 can be segmented into small mutually interdependent groups that are also well connected to other relatively autonomous parts of an organization. As a caution, however, these larger linked structures shouldn't be hierarchical but catalytic, supporting high rates of mutually accommodating interactions. Such systems will need some standard, easily understood protocols for clear communications. People will need to easily connect with each other no matter where in the world they happen to be.

These large, extended virtual networks should also offer ample opportunities for people to occasionally meet face-to-face. If face-to-face meetings aren't possible for all the network members, then at least periodic get-togethers should be arranged on a rotating basis among a significant portion of the participants. Recall that without in-person interactions, our hormones, neurotransmitters, and mirror, spindle, and oscillator brain cells have little chance of being fully engaged. This clearly implies that people in totally virtual networks will be unable to develop the close relationships and trust required for a meaningful shared identity.

Small size alone isn't enough to facilitate the emergence of an evocative shared identity essential for sustaining high levels of social capital and tacit knowledge sharing. I believe one of the most effective ways of developing unrestrained trust, interdependence, and robustness of a shared identity is through what I call "real teams."

Real teams are composed of volunteers since in an open self-organizing system no one makes assignments for someone else. People make their own commitments, knowing that their reputations depend on how well they keep those obligations. Team membership is usually quite diverse and includes a suitable mix of abilities, skills, and experiences. Each team member is well versed in group dynamics and participates fully in managing the overall team activities. People are free to join several teams, as long as they are able to fulfill their commitments to each team. Finally, every team keeps in touch with other teams throughout the enterprise to assure that all team activities are coordinated for the benefit of the whole organization.

Main points to keep in mind:

- *Face-to-face relationships.* Both human physiology and social needs demand at least periodic face-to-face codependent interactions between members of a group. Without that, a meaningful shared identity has little chance of emerging.
- *Interdependence and a sense of community.* The best way to develop and maintain a sense of community is through activities that benefit not only the enterprise as a whole but also each individual member.
- *Solidarity.* Members of a closely knit group need a sense of belonging.

- *Altruism and reciprocity.* People need to be willing to dedicate reasonable time and effort for the benefit of others knowing that over time such favors will be reciprocated.
- *Valued differences.* Associates need to appreciate diversity and knowing how to avoid groupthink.
- *Collective worldview.* Members need to share a meaningful interpretation of the biophysical and social environment that surrounds them.

Challenging Aspirations

An open, self-organizing system functions with voluntary cooperation and does not need a formalized structure and management controls, but it still needs a guidance structure. The third integrated principle provides the framework – an internal compass – that helps to keep all its members and teams advancing toward common goals without conventional management policies and directives.

Goals must give organizational affiliates much more than direction. They not only should be challenging, but they must also be inspiring. Establishing difficult targets is not the same as motivating people to reach for greater heights. In fact, it can be a hindrance to actual motivation and cause people to disengage.

Establishing challenging aspirations is a noncontrolling means to help people engage in self-organizing behaviors openly instead of covertly. Therefore, in a shared-access system, defining challenging and aspiring goals is a never-ending dynamic process involving all associates, where the focus is on both self-interest and mutual benefits.

The outcome of this continuous interdependent process is a living Challenging Aspirations document or inspiring vision statement containing all the mutually supportive goals of a shared-access ecology. Consequently, considerable time and effort needs to be devoted to developing and maintaining this document.

The Challenging Aspirations document would be similar to a corporate vision document, but with significant differences. Rather than being written by upper management, this document would be developed by all members of a group. In this way, all members would have ownership and would be committed to carrying it out. They would also feel empowered and willing to keep it updated to reflect current reality.

The document has two key components. One, it spells out the organizational goals that everyone has agreed to. Two, it is structured so that each member's aspirations are also contained in it. To be effective, it must be a synergistic document that spells out the benefits for both individuals and the organization as a whole. Every member of an enterprise needs to own it, be committed to supporting its aspirations in a balanced fashion.

In fact, the process of putting together the shared goals and getting total buy-in from all organizational members is at least as essential as the final product which, in reality, never is final. The principle of challenging aspirations is about developing goals that can satisfy both individual self-interests and mutual-interests without one impeding the attainment of the other. It is a delicate balancing act but well worth the effort.

To sum up, here are the main considerations for crafting a Shared Aspirations document:

- *Focus on possibilities.* There will always be problems to overcome. Payoffs, however, are greater in the pursuit of opportunities.
- *Equitable goals and incentives.* Assure that the quests of organizational goals are evenhandedly balanced with the interests of each member.
- *Periodic reflection.* This is not a waste of time. The process reassures that a venture and its members are on the same page and headed in an agreed upon direction.

Dynamic Organizational Alignment

Like sailing ships at sea, people and organizations occasionally get off course or even begin to drift aimlessly. When that occurs, those who first sight the danger immediately sound the alarm, alerting the rest of the crew to immediately take action and get back on course.

In a shared-access environment, there is no actual "captain" or mates to make major decisions or issue orders. Instead, every member of a self-organizing system must be a responsible crew member, prepared and willing to assume a leadership role, adapting to the problems or opportunities that surface, and keeping the organization on course. In other words, everyone becomes a catalytic leader helping to maintain the organization's dynamic alignment. Let's explore the meaning of these new terms.

Organizational alignment has nothing in common with maintaining control. It's all about sustaining dynamic order.

Dynamic order may sound like a contradiction in terms, but it is a result of catalytic leadership and circular causality. Remember that the properties of chaos dictate that a system is unpredictable and bounded at the same time, and that a system will never be in equilibrium, but will constantly shift to adapt to small changes. That's another way to describe a self-organizing system in dynamic alignment – it is unpredictable yet stays within its boundaries, and constantly adapts to changes.

So how does the catalytic leadership process of transparent decision-making help create dynamic organizational alignment?

Catalytic leadership is based on talent, skills, and experience rather than position power, so it takes considerably more energy, self-initiative, mental toughness, and never-ending persistence to work effectively in an overtly self-organizing environment. You have no place to hide; you are either in the game or out of it.

In a shared-access system, everybody takes full responsibility and accountability for the success or failure of the entire operation. Thus, to maintain or regain positive dynamic order, codependent decision-making and open dialogue are the most viable options in conjunction with shared leadership. This transparent-decision making is one of the necessary strategic tools that helps create dynamic organizational alignment.

It is also critical that all members of a shared-access environment practice interdependent thinking, which is a rather undeveloped skill for most of us. Perceiving wholes instead of individual parts or components isn't something most of us have learned to do in school or at work. Nor are most of us comfortable with sporadic, discontinuous change.

Overt self-organization, however, demands that all elements of a system be capable of functioning both autonomously and interdependently. Here again the focus is on complex adaptive systems rather than mechanistic, cause and effect models.

To sum up this part of the chapter, remember these major points about dynamic alignment:

- *Catalytic leadership.* People should ignore position power and practice codependent situational leadership.
- *Interdependent thinking.* Members must assure that everyone in the organization is aware of what everybody else is doing so that all actions contribute to the goals of the entire organization.
- *Transparent decisions.* Associates need to make sure that no one is left out of the decision-making loop.
- *Anticipate change.* All members should be geared to anticipate not only change but also discontinuous change around every corner and seek new possibilities to pursue.

UnManagement in Action

As depicted by Fig. 6.3, a shared-access system robustly improves an organization's ability to handle change by continuously expanding its shared-access domain and, as a natural consequence, its innovative capacity. The shared-access relationships exhibit tight interplay at three network levels: organizational, individual, and external.

At the organizational level, the principles supporting overt self-organization provide a nonthreatening and optimally supportive environment for the knowledge worker. It also gives members more than just monetary incentives. The shared-access context makes both individual autonomy and group responsibility integral factors in running the firm.

At the individual level, organizational affiliates can set and pursue their personal goals, take turns practicing catalytic leadership, and participate in the informal networks of their own choosing. Members can continuously expand their tacit and explicit knowledge.

Shared-access organizations are also interactive with valued external networks that support the challenging aspirations of the enterprise. In today's global environment,

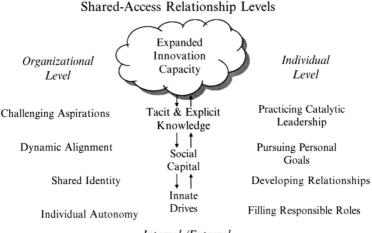

Fig. 6.3 Shared-access relationship levels

organizations can't prosper in relative isolation. They need to be on the constant lookout for people, institutions, and networks that may in some fashion contribute to their and future possibilities.

Clearly, it is a win-win situation at all three levels. In the final analysis, shared-access systems vigorously support the dynamic interplay of the triad – social capital, tacit knowledge, and our evolved genetic predispositions – in balanced fashion leading to increased coevolving relationships and increased innovation capacities.

In summary, consider the following attributes when developing shared-access ecologies:

- Recognize the unavoidable presence and influence of emergent social networks.
- Support the positive dynamics of personal triads and the shared-access domain by emphasizing:

    - Experimentation, discovery, and responsible risk taking
    - Shared goals and resource management
    - Open exchange of ideas and information
    - Valuing difference
    - Advancing common knowledge
    - Embracing discontinuous change
    - Promoting face-to-face interactions
    - Scheduling time for reflection
    - Supporting catalytic leadership

In the process of developing shared access, keep firmly in mind the fact that although "formal" structures and networks can be regulated or managed, the relationships between people that evolve within those structures and the expansion of the shared-access domain cannot. This means that no one can accurately predict the outcomes of any change initiatives. Therefore, all systems need to be continually "fine tuned" by the people actually engaged in the day-to-day activities. They are the only folks capable of expanding or contracting the most productive area of an organization or network, the shared-access domain.

The reason for that is simple. The shared-access domain is wholly founded on self-organization. Hence, it can be influenced by environmental context that surrounds it, but it can't be managed.

For the very same reason, "outside entities" such as management consultants should not implement change initiatives. Getting advice from consultants is all well and good, but acceptance and implementation of the changes they propose should be entrusted to the people who actually do the work.

If that's not the case, the informal social networks will only give lip service to the new schemes or worse undermine them. That is, the informal networks may or may not support the overall goals and initiatives proposed by the consultants or management.

Thus, you have come full circle and, in essence, created another controlled-access system, not a shared-access ecology.

This is usually exactly what happens with most change programs. Without purposefully creating shared-access as part of the program, some change may be affected in the system, but the overall relationships stay much the same. As the well-known neuroscientists Cacioppo and Patrick (2008, p. 222) suggest:

When we feel safe and secure within our social connections, we can move along free of bias and unwarranted expectations. Relaxed and attentive, we can be in sync with the movements of others. With no expectations that we'll be excluded our defensive, fight or flight mechanisms are not on the ready alert. Free from all this distraction, we are able to detect more reliably whether any budding connection is promising or an invitation to the blues. Living more calmly in the moment, we can make better choices. Which has the added benefit of helping improve our larger social environment over time.

Some Concerns

Let me conclude this chapter with an interesting scenario that appears to indicate we have a long way to go before most management consultants, executives, and educators begin to realize the "hidden power" of emergent networks and codependent relationships. Unfortunately, it also demonstrates why the development of shared-access organizational ecologies will not be on top of most boardroom meeting agendas in the near future.

James Cash, Michael Earl, and Robert Morison (2008, p. 92) state in their recent *Harvard Business Review* article, "Teaming Up to Crack Innovation Enterprise Integration," that "Businesses are better at stifling innovation than capitalizing on it, better at optimizing local operations than integrating them for the good of the enterprise and customers. The larger and more complex the organization, the stronger the status quo can be in repelling both innovation and integration." Bravo! I couldn't have said it better myself.

Given their great statement, however, I was amazed at what these sage individuals propose as remedies. They suggest that large businesses should add two more offices or departments to the already complex bureaucratic systems to better "share skills, experiences, and insights across the silos." One group would "combine a company's own innovation efforts with the best of external technology to create new business variations." The other entity would fold "yesterday's new variations into the operating model of the enterprise."

Obviously, the ideas look good on paper. However, if many of the workers in an organization are already disengaged, have few codependent relationships, and have difficulty maintaining their identities, is it realistic to think that two more formal groups will solve the innovation and integration problem?

Hardly! First, there needs to be a well developed shared-access organizational context that not only supports the growth of member triads but also the expansion of the shared-access domain within the enterprise. Unfortunately, if such changes don't take place first then the status quo will mostly likely remain firmly in place.

References

Block, P. (2008) *Community: The Structure of Belonging*. San Francisco: *Berrett-Koehle*r.

Cacioppo, J. T. and Patrick, W. (2008) *Lonliness*. New York: W. W. Norton and Company.

Cash, J. I., Earl, M. E. and Morison, R. (2008) "Teaming Up to Crack Innovation Enterprise Integration." *Harvard Business Review*, November, pp. 90–100.

Dunbar, R. (1996) *Grooming, Gossip, and the Evolution of Language*. Cambridge: Harvard University Press.

Ehin, C. (2005) *Hidden Assets: Harnessing the Power of Informal Networks*. New York: Springer.

Gaba, V. and Meyer, A. D. (2008) "Crossing the Organizational Species Barrier: How Venture Capital Practices Infiltrated the Information Technology Sector." *The Academy of Management Journal*, Vol. 51, Nr. 5, pp. 976–998.

Gleick, J. (1988) *Chaos: Making a New Science*. New York: Penguin Books.

Goleman, D. and Boyatzis, R. (2008) "Social Intelligence and the Biology of Leadership." *Harvard Business Review*, September, pp. 74–81.

Smith, C. and Comer, D. (1994) "Self-Organization in Small Groups." *Human Relations*, Vol. 47, Nr. 5, pp. 553–581.

Stacey, R. D., Griffin, D. and Shaw, P. (2000) *Complexity and Management: Fad or Radical Challenge to Systems Thinking?* New York: Routledge.

Tierney, J. (2008) "As Barriers Disappear, Some Gender Gaps Widen." *The New York Times*, September 9, p. F1.

Waldrop, M. M. (1992) *Complexity*. New York: Simon & Schuster

Watts, D. J. (2003) *Six Degrees*. New York: W. W. Norton.

Chapter 7
Epilogue: Living on the Edge

"There are no guarantees in life."

The irony is that we ignore this well-known sage observation in most of our organizations. We expect everything to run like clockwork as neatly prescribed by all sorts of regulations, policies, and vision statements.

Consequently, we end up not only disappointed when things don't turn out as expected, but also puzzled how work gets done despite all the apparent problems. But as we've seen, it really isn't that much of a mystery.

The relationship factors we've explored are both life sustaining and nondeterministic, and their interrelated dynamics are both unpredictable and limitless. No one can control or manage these relationship factors to bring about a particular outcome because there simply is nothing tangible to manipulate. You only have the intrinsic, emergent, receptive, and intangible processes of creating relationships at play.

All living systems constantly self-organize in response to the conditions of their immediate surroundings. Self-organization or circular causality is an emergent process of attraction and repulsion in which the system's complexity changes without outside interference.

The bottom line is that self-organization begins at the molecular level of every organic entity, including humans, and extends outward to their contact with the outside world.

What this also implies is that not only are relationships formed by self-organization, but also by the emergence and maintenance of individual personal identities. Accordingly, people need to have the freedom to explore and interact within their immediate environments to find their specific footing. They also need to discover, based on their talents and experiences, what roles they can meaningfully assume in varying social settings.

With this knowledge, it becomes understandable why so many people are disengaged at their places of work. As stated before, how can a person be engaged when the work contexts in many organizations seldom allow them to find their niche or maintain their personal identity?

C. Ehin, *The Organizational Sweet Spot: Engaging the Innovative Dynamics of Your Social Networks*, DOI 10.1007/978-0-387-98194-9_7, © Springer Science + Business Media, LLC 2009

Consequently, we need to discover how to promote the limitless power of our emergent social networks within and external to our enterprises. That, I believe, can be accomplished best by finding the "sweet spot" or the "shared-access domain" within every organization as depicted in Fig. 2.4 in Chap. 2.

Once members of an organization become aware of the sweet spot, they can act strategically to expand this productive and innovative zone. More informal networks voluntarily participate in the implicit coordination of the organization's productive activities as the sweet spot expands.

At the same time, the explicit coordination and control elements of the formal organizational framework begin to recede, eventually becoming significantly reduced. The people become less managed and more engaged.

The power of such social engagement can provide tremendous results as portrayed in Fig. 7.1. That power emanates from the simultaneous, mutually supportive interactions between the individuals. In the process, people grow, their triads expand further, and the network as a whole gains more and more innovative capacity and capability. Transactions and conversations are important, but emergent and expanding relationships give social engagements their unbounded power.

Clearly, this circular progression squarely rests on the desire of each network member to engage each other as fully as possible, thus expanding the shared-access domain to its maximum limits. What should also be apparent is that the dynamics of neither the individual elements nor the framework as a whole can be managed in the traditional sense.

Three critical factors must be present to breathe life into such a complex vibrant structure:

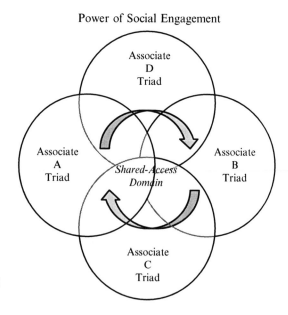

Fig. 7.1 Power of social engagement

- Assembling a group of about 150 people with the right talents, knowledge, and social predispositions for a particular venture
- Allowing group members to select worthy and challenging possibilities to pursue or problems to solve
- Assisting the group to develop a constructive social context where they can practice a mix of moderate self-interests and outward-reaching altruism.

Successful installation of all three factors will lead to the desirable expansion of the shared-access domain with its high sustained levels of embedded engagements.

Keep in mind that organizational structures can be adjusted and managed. However, the effects these modifications will have on informal social networks can't be precisely predicted or controlled. As a result, the catalytic leadership, expert power, and emergent relationships of its members will determine how an organization evolves. One individual or a small group of people wielding position power will have much less effect on what the organization looks like.

Whether we like to admit it or not, all activities and interactions between people are governed by the principles of self-organization. Therefore, we need to place greater emphasis on developing constructive social contexts that support these dynamics. We need to allow people to establish meaningful relationships rather than focusing mainly on transactions, minimizing conversations, and almost completely ignoring relationships.

Ideally, let's not stop at organizations. Engaging the workforce to the fullest extent possible shouldn't only be the objective of every business, but society as a whole. Instead of wasting hundreds of billions of dollars a year primarily on financial transactions and minimizing conversations we could invest that money in education and offer higher salaries to our workers.

Unfortunately, that may only happen after a significant number of executives begin to accept that the more an institution supports the principles of self-organization *openly*, the more it will benefit from increased innovation and expansion of knowledge through activation of innate individual attention, social capital, and tacit knowledge sharing among its members.

Thus, the primary emphasis should be on "unmanagement" rather than the continuous refinement of top-down administrative schemes. Most heads of organizations, however, still have difficulty grasping that by giving up control managers will actually gain more control. It's all about understanding the uncontrollable self-organizing dynamics of complex evolving social entities. There seems to be nothing in our evolutionary past that suggests we were meant to be managed by others. If that were not so, we modern humans probably would never have made it this far.

Regrettably, there are hundreds of consultants around the world ready to offer solutions, often costly and ultimately useless. Of course, many of these experts can be out of touch with the latest developments in their respective fields, but they still try to dazzle you with their multicolored charts and models. This poses considerable risk to high-tech professionals who are constantly on the lookout for new ideas and methods.

Being out of touch isn't limited to the province of consultants alone. We can all at times be afflicted with this debilitating but seldom acknowledged condition. Let me suggest why this state of mind can be quite common.

First, we know it is physiologically impossible for any one of us to see, perceive, learn, and understand something (e.g., an object, theory, person, etc.) exactly the same way as any other person because two people are *exactly* identical. Everyone perceives the world around them a little differently than everyone else. As a result, we all have our own individual theories and assumptions (tacit knowledge) that helps guide us through life.

Second, the more successful we are in our activities following our world views, the more we tend to depend on them. In the end our viewpoints can become fossilized or written in stone. Classic examples are a plethora of leadership and management principles still in use, even though time and new evidence has proven many of them to be ineffective or even counterproductive.

Finally, people who eventually attain high levels of recognition either through key leadership positions, consulting, or scholarship are often marked as authorities or "gurus" in their particular fields and their opinions carry an inordinate amount of weight. Eventually, however, their principles can also become fossilized if they aren't aware of or open to change as new knowledge is introduced.

Seven ways to spot and avoid being bamboozled by individuals and who may be out of touch are:

- *Research is considered a waste of time.* "We have been very successful and our experience speaks for itself."
- *Lack of critical thinking.* "That may work well within such and such an organization, but we are different."
- *An inability to take constructive criticism and lack of respect for varied opinions.* "We are the originators of this method/product/theory. Who are they/you to question us?"
- *Maintaining a positive image at all cost.* "What would people think of us if this didn't work as expected?"
- *Lack of effective practice.* "We have been advised by the best minds in the business. We can skip the experimental phase."
- *Blind faith in experts and top executives.* "How can we go wrong? These people have worked with the top companies around the world for years."
- *An aversion to introspection.* "We don't need that fuzzy self-examination of feelings, thoughts and motives around here. We are practical people."

We all occasionally lose touch. The best approach in avoiding it is to use caution as we go through cycles of developing, modifying, and replacing various management theories. No matter what conceptual framework we come up with, we should be keenly aware that something new will eventually replace or modify the older models.

To avoid losing touch and becoming complacent, I suggest that we try to "live on the edge" as much as possible. When I say "live on the edge" I don't mean we should binge at wild parties every night, bungee jump off bridges, or race in the Indianapolis 500.

Rather, my sense of living on the edge means pushing the limits of biophysical and social knowledge. That's why one of the first things I do in the morning after my morning routine is to scan the Science section of a major news publication with several questions in mind. Has there been a recent new discovery? Has someone put a new twist on an assumption that's been around for years? How do all these things relate to my mental models? How do I need to redefine or adjust my assumptions about the world in general? And, most importantly, "How do I apply what I've just learned?"

We should question ourselves daily to push the boundaries of our knowledge and constantly update and expand our own individual triads. Of course, this type of living on the edge also helps to support the expansion of the shared-access domains of our places of work and in all our social networks.

In the final analysis, living on the edge means that we should strive to continuously answer on overall key question: "What one seemingly impossible thing today would immensely improve our lives IF it could be made possible?"

Be able to ask that question is what it means to me to live on the edge or push the envelope. Can you imagine how much energy and power for positive change we could generate if we all regularly pursued answers to that very question?

Thus, I ask you to take another "critical" but open mined look at the nonprescriptive models I've assembled in this book. See if they can be helpful guides, as opposed to prescriptions, in exploring future possibilities. We can begin to make it possible.

In looking for answers and possibilities, be cautious about using "benchmarks" too extensively. Taking a close look at what other people are doing has its merits, but always remember that copying exactly what your adversaries or friends are doing won't get you far. Benchmarks, like case studies, are good history lessons. History, however, almost never repeats itself exactly the same way. Accordingly, the most meaningful payoffs are usually found in the exceptions to the rules.

Below are what I consider to be the most important "unmanagement" principles to keep in mind as we scan the horizon for new possibilities and ventures:

- Organizational context parameters can be adjusted and managed.
- Relationships and identities are emergent and their outcomes can't be accurately predicted, no less managed.
- Coevolving relationships are founded on interdependence and mutual trust.
- Identities are founded on people's perceptions and their attributes are related to specific contexts.
- Relationships of organizational members determine what a venture becomes.
- Systems designed to marshal group efforts and intelligence should be based on self-organizing principles not cause and effect thinking.

Also, try to remember the three primary factors and their specific attributes influencing the activities of the shared-access domain:

- The formal system equates to control and profits.
- The shared-access domain equates to productive dynamic order.
- The informal networks equate to relationships and identities.

Again, what stands out above is that only the formal system can be "managed." Neither the shared-access domain nor the informal networks can be managed because they are "emergent." They can, however, be influenced. The formal system needs to be constantly "fine tuned," but not just by management. It is vital to actively engage as many members of an organization as possible to ensure expansion of individual Triads as well as the shared-access domain. Always aim for the sweet spot!

A sage old Chinese proverb captures the essence of the engagement process perfectly:

Tell me, I'll forget.

Show me, I may remember.

Involve me, I'll understand.

Genuine engagement of people now and throughout the history of our kind on our Blue Planet has been the key to survival and success. May we continue to pursue positive engagement for the betterment of ourselves, our organizations, and all our global neighbors.

Appendix A
Identifying the Controlled-Access Context[1]

Maintaining Order and Control

Leadership is based on position power. Most activities are expected to be predictable, controlled, and operating at optimum efficiency.

- Only a few key individuals have the responsibility and authority to maintain control by developing, clarifying, and reinforcing goals, action plans, and policies. Their task is to identify problems and prescribe solutions.
- Everyone is expected to diligently follow prescribed rules and behavioral guidelines in addition to embracing the solutions to the problems presented by management.
- All changes are made incrementally by the direction of upper management following rigorous formal planning and the establishment of precise implementation guidelines.
- Everyone is *asked* and *expected* to be a team player in addition to being dedicated to formally communicated cultural values.

Work Practices

Goals and objectives are the purview of Management. People have little autonomy in redesigning work contexts that may be more challenging and rewarding.

- Education and training are primarily geared toward making current jobs more efficient and predictable.
- Little value is placed on developing and maintaining a sense of community that emphasizes intimacy, trust, and mutual support.
- Few people have line-of-sight relationships with other organizational groups or customer.

---

[1] Adapted from Charles Ehin, *Unleashing Intellectual Capital* (Butterworth-Heinemann, 2000).

- Most people are not expected to understand the socially significant purpose and the overall interconnected operations of the business.
- Individuals and teams are seldom asked for input regarding how organizational activities, resources, and rewards should be managed.

Frequently Heard Comments

- You must.
- That's not my job.
- You have no choice.
- Have you forgotten the deadline?
- We need to talk.
- It's the bottom line that counts.
- This is for your own good.
- Get off my back.
- I don't care how you feel.
- You had better pay attention to company policy.
- Don't you understand?
- Is it time to go home yet?

Appendix B
Identifying the Shared-Access Context[1]

Maintaining Order and Control

Leadership is based on expertise and social attention holding potential (catalytic leadership) with emphasis on individual commitment and dynamic interconnectedness.

- Proper direction is attained and maintained through a shared identity and self-reference and not by conformity or "herd mentality." It is unity expressed through diversity.
- Everything is open to constant examination, experimentation, and improvement.
- Change is part of the everyday process. The organization is intended to operate on the edge of chaos, never in a stable, fixed point but continuously evolving in response to an unpredictable and changing environment.
- Organizational members are considered to be *partners* responsible and accountable for both individual and collective activities.

Work Practices

Most activities are based on reciprocal relationships, valued differences, and respected individual identities. Emphasis is placed on constant examination and experimentation that may lead to more challenging and rewarding networked processes.

- A strong belief that organizational strength stems from the synchronized efforts of extraordinary people is evident. Consequently, everyone is expected to continuously attain new competencies that benefit not only the company but also the growth and worth of each individual member.
- Every opportunity is taken to strengthen the sense of community through mutually beneficial activities, interactions, and the sharing of sentiments.

---

[1] Adapted from Charles Ehin, *Unleashing Intellectual Capital* (Butterworth-Heinemann, 2000).

- The pursuit of creativity and innovation is enhanced through the persistent encouragement of constructive dissent in an atmosphere of mutual trust.
- Complex adaptive systems' thinking is pervasive. Interconnectedness of all proposed actions and continuing activities are diligently scrutinized to ensure effective common results.
- Every member is actively engaged in assuring that all activities, resources, and rewards are equitably managed.

Frequently Heard Comments

- Can you think of other options?
- Am I on the right track?
- Let's take another look at that deadline.
- Thanks for taking the initiative.
- How often should we meet?
- We're in it together.
- What's your gut feeling on this?
- How can I help?
- Is this mutually beneficial?
- How does this support our overall activities?
- Please take a real critical look at my proposal.
- How time flies.

Bibliography

Adler, P. S. and Seok-Woo, K. (2002) "Social Capital: Prospects for a New Concept." *The Academy of Management Review*, Vol. 27, Nr. 1, pp. 17–40.

Allee, V. (2003) *The Future of Knowledge*. Boston: Butterworth-Heinemann.

Allen, S., Deragon, J. T., Orem, M. G. and Smith, C. F. (2008) *The Emergence of the Relationship Economy*. Cupertino, CA: HappyAbout.Info.

Baily, K. (1987) *Human Paleopsychology: Applications to Aggression and Pathological Processes*. Hillsdale, NJ: Hove and London.

Barkow, J. H., Cosmides, L. and Toomby, J. (1995) *The Adapted Mind: Evolutionary Psychology and the Generation of Culture*. New York: Oxford University Press.

Bedeian, A. G. (2002) "The Dean's Disease: How the Dark Side of Power Manifests Itself in the Office of Dean." *Academy of Management Learning & Education*, December, Vol. 1, Nr. 2, pp. 164–173.

Berntson, G. G. and Cacioppo, J. T. (2008) The Neuroevolution of Motivation. In J. Shah and W. Gardner (Eds.), Handbook of Motivation Science. New York: Guilford, pp. 188–200.

Birkinshaw, J., Hamel, G. and Mol, M. J. (2008) "Management Innovation." *The Academy of Management Review*, Vol. 33, Nr. 4, pp. 825–845.

Block, P. (1993) *Stewardship: Choosing Service over Self-Interest*. San Francisco: Berrett-Koehler.

Block, P. (2008) *Community: The Structure of Belonging*. San Francisco: Berrett-Koehler.

Boon, L. E. and Bowen, D. D. (1987) *The Great Writings in Management and Organizational Behavior*. New York: Random House.

Cacioppo, J. T. and Patrick, W. (2008) *Lonliness*. New York: W. W. Norton and Company.

Camazine, S., Deneubourg, J., Franks, N. R., Sneyd, J., Theraulaz, G. and Bonabeau, E. *Self-Organization in Biological Systems*. Princeton: Princeton University Press.

Cash, J. I., Earl, M. E. and Morison, R. (2008) "Teaming Up to Crack Innovation Enterprise Integration." *Harvard Business Review*, November, pp. 90–100.

Collins, J. (2002) *Good to Great*. New York: Harper Business.

Dawkins, R. (2005) *The Ancestor's Tale*. New York: Houghton Mifflin.

Dunbar, R. (1996) *Grooming, Gossip, and the Evolution of Language*. Cambridge: Harvard University Press.

Edelman, G. M. (1992) *Bright Air, Brilliant Fire*. New York: Harper Collins.

Ehin, C. (2000) *Unleashing Intellectual Capital*. Boston: Butterworth-Heinemann.

Ehin, C. (2005) *Hidden Assets: Harnessing the Power of Informal Networks*. Boston: Springer.

English, F. W. (2008) *The Art of Educational Leadership*. Thousand Oaks, CA: Sage.

Friedman, T. L. (2008) *Hot, Flat, and Crowded*. New York: Farrar, Straus and Giroux.

Gaba, V. and Meyer, A. D. (2008) "Crossing the Organizational Species Barrier: How Venture Capital Practices Infiltrated the Information Technology Sector." *The Academy of Management Journal*, Vol. 51, Nr. 5, pp. 976–998.

George, C. S. (1972) *The History of Management Thought*. Englewood Cliffs, NJ: Prentice-Hall.

Gigerenzer, G. (2007) *Gut Feelings: The Intelligence of the Unconscious*. New York: Viking.

Gladwell, M. (2008) *Outliers*. New York: Little, Brown and Company.

Gleick, J. (1988) *Chaos: Making a New Science*. New York: Penguin Books.

Goleman, D. and Boyatzis, R. (2008) "Social Intelligence and the Biology of Leadership." *Harvard Business Review*, September, pp. 74–81.

Goleman, D., Boyatzis, R. and McKee, (2001) "Primal Leadership: The Hidden Driver of Great Performance." *Harvard Business Review*, December, pp. 42-51.

Hallowell, E. M. (1999) "The Human Moment at Work." *Harvard Business Review*, January–February, pp. 58–66.

Kelso, J. A. S. (1995) *Dynamic Patterns: The Self-Organization of Brain and Behavior*. Cambridge, MA: MIT Press.

Kluger, J. (2007) "What Makes Us Moral." *Time*, December 3, pp. 54-60.

Kluger, J. (2008) *Simplexity: How Simple Things Become Complex*. New York: Hyperion.

Le Doux, J. (2002) *Synaptic Self: How Our Brains Become Who We Are*. New YorkPenguin Books.

Levine, F., Locke, C., Searls, D. and Weinberger, D. (2000) *The Cluetrain Manifesto: The End of Business as Usual*. Cambridge, MA: Perseus.

Linden, D. (2007) *The Accidental Mind*. Cambridge: Harvard University Press.

Lynch, G. and Granger, R. (2008) *Big Brain: The Origin and Future of Human Intelligence*. New York: Palgrave Macmillan.

MacLean, P. D. (1973) *A Triune Concept of the Brain Behavior*. Toronto: University of Toronto Press.

Marcus, G. (2008) *Kluge: The Haphazard Construction of the Human Mind*. New York: Houghton Mifflin.

Medina, J. (2008) *Brain Rules*. Seattle: Pear.

Montague, R. (2006) *Why Choose This Book? How We Make Decisions*. New York Dutton.

Morris, H. J. (2001) "Happiness Explained." *U.S. News & World Report*, September 3, pp. 46–54.

Nahapiet, J. and Ghoshal, S. (1998) "Social Capital, Intellectual Capital, and the Organizational Advantage." *The Academy of Management Review*, March, pp. 242–266.

Nicholson, N. (2008) "Evolutionary Psychology, Organizational Culture, and the Family Firm." *Academy of Management Perspectives*, May, Vol. 22, Nr. 2, pp. 73–84.

Pierce, J. L. and Newstrom, J. W. (2000) *Leaders and the Leadership Process*. New York: McGraw-Hill.

Pinker, S. (2002) *The Blank Slate: The Modern Denial of Human Nature*. New York: Viking.

Polanyi, M. (1958) *Personal Knowledge*. Chicago: University of Chicago Press.

Putnam, R., Feldstein, L. M. and Cohen, D. (2003) *Better Together: Restoring the American Community*. New York: Simon & Schuster.

Ridley, M. (2003) *Nature via Nurture*. New York: Harper Collins.

Rubin, H. (1999) "Only the Pronoid Survive." *Fast Company*, November.

Sagan, C. (1977) *The Dragons of Eden*. New York: Random House.

Scanlan, B. K. (1981) "Creating a Climate for Achievement." *Business Horizons*, March–April, pp. 5–9.

Schoderbek, P. P., Schoderbek, C. G. and Kefalas, A. G. (1990) *Management Systems*. Boston, MA: Richard D. Irwin.

Searls, D. (2007) *Weblog*, December 26.

Senge, P. (1990) "The Leader's New Work: Building Learning Organizations." *Sloan Management Review*, Fall, pp. 7-23.

Senge, P., Smith, B., Kruschwitz, N., Laur, J. and Schley, S. (2008) *The Necessary Revolution*. New York: Doubleday.

Shubin, N. (2008) *Your Inner Fish*. New York: Pantheon Books.

Smith, C. and Comer, D. (1994) "Self-Organization in Small Groups." *Human Relations*, Vol. 47, 533–581Nr. 5.

Snowden, D. J. and Boone, M. E. (2007) "A Leader's Framework for Decision Making." Harvard Business Review, November, pp. 68–76.

Stacey, R. D., Griffin, D. and Shaw, P. (2000) *Complexity and Management: Fad or Radical Challenge to Systems Thinking?* New York: Routledge.

Sternberg, R. and Horvath, J. (Eds.) (1999) *Tacit Knowledge in Professional Practices: Researcher and Practitioner Perspectives*. Mahwah, NJ: Lawrence Erlbaum.

Stevens, A. and Price, T. (1996) *Evolutionary Psychiatry: A New Beginning*. New York: Routledge.

Taleb, N. N. (2007) *The Black Swan: The Impact of the Highly Improbable*. New York: Random House.

Waldrop, M. M. (1992) *Complexity*. New York: Simon & Schuster.

Watts, D. J. (2003) *Six Degrees*. New York: W. W. Norton.

White, H. (2008) *Identity and Control*. Princeton: Princeton University Press.

White, H. C. and Godart, F. C. (2003) "Stories from Identity and Control." *Sociologica*, March, Nr. 3, pp. 1–17, 10.2383/25960.

Wilson, E. O. (1998) *Consilience: The Unity of Knowledge*. New York: Knopf.

Zahra, S. A. and George, G. (2002) "Absorptive Capacity: A Review, Reconceptualization, and Extension." *The Academy of Management Review*, April, Vol. 27, Nr. 2, pp. 185–203.

About the Author

Professor Charles (Kalev) Ehin is an accomplished author and recognized management authority. He is currently an emeritus professor of management at Westminster College in Salt Lake City, UT where he also served as the Dean of the Gore School of Business. After retiring from the US Air Force, where he held various leadership positions and taught at the Air Command and Staff College, and prior to joining Westminster College, he worked as an internal organization development consultant in the private sector.

Dr. Ehin was born in Estonia and during World War II his family was torn apart by the disastrous struggle for supremacy in Europe by two dictatorships, Nazi Germany and the Soviet Union. In 1950 he was finally able to emigrate to the USA. The tragic events that he and his family experienced during the course of the war and their everlasting affects are chronicled in his book, *Aftermath* (Publish America, 2004).

Professor Ehin is also the author of several groundbreaking management books. *Unleashing Intellectual Capital* (Butterworth-Heinemann, 2000 - now available from Elsevier) broke new ground by introducing the duality of human nature to the realm of management and its impact on differing organizational contexts. His follow-on work, *Hidden Assets: Harnessing the Power of Informal Networks* (Springer, 2004), makes it quite clear why people can be physically controlled but not managed. *The Organizational Sweet Spot: Engaging the Innovative Dynamics of Your Social Networks* (Springer, 2009) pinpoints where most of the work in an enterprise takes place and how that "sweet spot" can be expanded.

Index